Wood and Forest

by William Noyes

FOREWORD

This book has been prepared as a companion volume to the author's Handwork in Wood.[1] It is an attempt to collect and arrange in available form useful information, now widely scattered, about our common woods, their sources, growth, properties and uses.

As in the other volume, the credit for the successful completion of the book is to be given to my wife, Anna Gausmann Noyes, who has made the drawings and maps, corrected the text, read the proof, and carried the work thru to its final completion.

Acknowledgments are hereby thankfully made for corrections and suggestions in the text to the following persons:

Mr. A. D. Hopkins, of the United States Department of Agriculture, Bureau of Entomology, for revision of the text relating to Insect Enemies of the Forest, in Chapter VI.

Mr. George G. Hedgcock, of the United States Bureau of Agriculture, Bureau of Plant Industry, for revision of the text relating to the fungal enemies of the forest, in Chapter VI.

Mr. S. T. Dana and Mr. Burnett Barrows, of the United States Department of Agriculture, Forest Service, for revision of Chapters IV, V, VI, VII, and VIII.

Professor Charles R. Richards, formerly Head of the Manual Training Department of Teachers College, my predecessor as lecturer of the course out of which this book has grown.

Professor M. A. Bigelow, Head of the Department of Botany of Teachers College, for revision of Chapter I, on the Structure of Wood.

Mr. Romeyn B. Hough, of Lowville, N. Y., author of American Woods and Handbook of the Trees of the Northern States and Canada, for suggestions in preparing the maps in Chapter III.

The Forest Service, Washington, D. C., for photographs and maps credited to it, and for permission to reprint the key to the identification of woods which appears in Forest Service Bulletin No. 10, Timber, by Filibert Roth.

The Division of Publications, U. S. Department of Agriculture, for permission to copy illustrations in bulletins.

The Macmillan Company, New York, for permission to reproduce Fig. 86, Portion of the Mycelium of Dry Rot, from Timber and Some of its Diseases, by H. M. Ward.

Mrs. Katharine Golden Bitting, of Lafayette, Indiana, for the photograph of the cross-section of a bud, Figure 5.

Finally and not least I hereby acknowledge my obligations to the various writers and publishers whose books and articles I have freely used. As far as possible, appropriate credit is given in the paged references at the end of each chapter.

CONTENTS.

CHAPTER

CHAPTER I.

THE STRUCTURE OF WOOD.

When it is remembered that the suitability of wood for a particular purpose depends most of all upon its internal structure, it is plain that the woodworker should know the essential characteristics of that structure. While his main interest in wood is as lumber, dead material to be used in woodworking, he can properly understand its structure only by knowing something of it as a live, growing organism. To facilitate this, a knowledge of its position in the plant world is helpful.

All the useful woods are to be found in the highest sub-kingdom of the plant world, the flowering plants or Phanerogamia of the botanist. These flowering plants are to be classified as follows:

{ I. Gymnosperms. (Naked seeds.) { 1. Cycadaceae. (Palms, ferns, etc.) { 2. Gnetaceae. (Joint firs.) { 3. Conifers. Pines, firs, etc. Phanerogamia, { II.

Angiosperms. (Fruits.) (Flowering plants) { 1. Monocotyledons. (One seed-leaf.) { (Palms, bamboos, grasses, etc.) { 2. Dicotyledons. (Two seed-leaves.) { a. Herbs. { b. Broad-leaved trees.

Under the division of naked-seeded plants (gymnosperms), practically the only valuable timber-bearing plants are the needle-leaved trees or the conifers, including such trees as the pines, cedars, spruces, firs, etc. Their wood grows rapidly in concentric annual rings, like that of the broad-leaved trees; is easily worked, and is more widely used than the wood of any other class of trees.

Of fruit-bearing trees (angiosperms), there are two classes, those that have one seed-leaf as they germinate, and those that have two seed-leaves.

The one seed-leaf plants (monocotyledons) include the grasses, lilies, bananas, palms, etc. Of these there are only a few that reach the dimensions of trees. They are strikingly distinguished by the structure of their stems. They have no cambium layer and no distinct bark and pith; they have unbranched stems, which as a rule do not increase in diameter after the first stages of growth, but grow only terminally. Instead of having concentric annual rings and thus growing larger year by year, the woody tissue grows here and there thru the stem, but mostly crowded together toward the outer surfaces. Even where there is radial growth, as in yucca, the structure is not in annual rings, but irregular. These one seed-leaf trees (monocotyledons) are not of much economic value as lumber, being used chiefly "in the round," and to some extent for veneers and inlays; e.g., cocoanut-palm and porcupine wood are so used.

The most useful of the monocotyledons, or endogens, ("inside growers," as they are sometimes called,) are the bamboos, which are giant members of the group of grasses, Fig. 1. They grow in dense forests, some varieties often 70 feet high and 6 inches in diameter, shooting up their entire height in a single season. Bamboo is very highly valued in the Orient, where it is used for masts, for house rafters, and other building purposes, for gutters and water-pipes and in countless other ways. It is twice as strong as any of our woods.

Under the fruit-bearing trees (angiosperms), timber trees are chiefly found among those that have two seed-leaves (the dicotyledons) and include the great mass of broad-leaved or deciduous trees such as chestnut, oak, ash and maple. It is to these and to the conifers that our principal attention will be given, since they constitute the bulk of the wood in common use.

The timber-bearing trees, then, are the:

(1) Conifers, the needle-leaved, naked-seeded trees, such as pine, cedar, etc. Fig. 45, p. 199.

(2) Endogens, which have one seed-leaf, such as bamboos, Fig. 1.

(3) Broad-leaved trees, having two seed-leaves, such as oak, beech, and elm. Fig. 48, p. 202.

The common classifications of trees are quite inaccurate. Many of the so-called deciduous (Latin, deciduus, falling off) trees are evergreen, such as holly, and, in the south, live oak, magnolia and cherry. So, too, some of the alleged "evergreens," like bald cypress and tamarack, shed their leaves annually.

Not all of the "conifers" bear cones. For example, the juniper bears a berry. The ginko, Fig. 2, tho classed among the "conifers," the "evergreens," and the "needle-leaf" trees, bears no cones, has broad leaves and is deciduous. It has an especial interest as being the sole survivor of many species which grew abundantly in the carboniferous age.

Also, the terms used by lumbermen, "hard woods" for broad-leaved trees and "soft woods" for conifers, are still less exact, for the wood of some broad-leaved trees, as bass and poplar, is much softer than that of some conifers, as Georgia pine and lignum vitae.

Another classification commonly made is that of "endogens" (inside growers) including bamboos, palms, etc., and exogens (outside growers) which would include both conifers and broad-leaved trees.

One reason why so many classifications have come into use is that none of them is quite accurate. A better one will be explained later. See p. 23.

As in the study of all woods three sections are made, it is well at the outset to understand clearly what these are.

The sections of a tree made for its study are (Fig. 3):

(1) Transverse, a plane at right angles to the organic axis.

(2) Radial, a longitudinal plane, including the organic axis.

A.

A, B, C, D, Transverse Section. B, D, E, F, Radial Section. G, H, I, J, Tangential Section.

B.

A, B, C, Transverse Section. A, B, D, E, Radial Section. B, C, E, F, Tangential Section.]

(3) Tangential, a longitudinal plane not including the organic axis.

If a transverse section of the trunk of a conifer or of a broad-leaved tree is made, it is to be noted that it consists of several distinct parts. See Fig. 4. These, beginning at the outside, are:

(1) Rind or bark (a) Cortex (b) Bast

(2) Cambium

(3) Wood (a) Sap-wood (b) Heart-wood

(4) Pith.

(1) The rind or bark is made up of two layers, the outer of which, the "cortex," is corky and usually scales or pulls off easily; while the inner one is a fibrous coat called "bast" or "phloem." Together they form a cone, widest, thickest, and roughest at the base and becoming narrower toward the top of the tree. The cortex or outer bark serves to protect the stem of the tree from

extremes of heat and cold, from atmospheric changes, and from the browsing of animals. It is made up of a tough water-proof layer of cork which has taken the place of the tender skin or "epidermis" of the twig. Because it is water-proof the outside tissue is cut off from the water supply of the tree, and so dries up and peels off, a mass of dead matter. The cork and the dead stuff together are called the bark. As we shall see later, the cork grows from the inside, being formed in the inner layers of the cortex, the outer layers of dry bark being thus successively cut off.

The characteristics of the tree bark are due to the positions and kinds of tissue of these new layers of cork. Each tree has its own kind of bark, and the bark of some is so characteristic as to make the tree easily recognizable.

Bark may be classified according to formation and method of separation, as scale bark, which detaches from the tree in plates, as in the willows; membraneous bark, which comes off in ribbons and films, as in the birches; fibrous bark, which is in the form of stiff threads, as in the grape vine; and fissured bark, which breaks up in longitudinal fissures, showing ridges, grooves and broad, angular patches, as in oak, chestnut and locust. The last is the commonest form of bark.

The bark of certain kinds of trees, as cherry and birch, has peculiar markings which consist of oblong raised spots or marks, especially on the young branches. These are called lenticels (Latin lenticula, freckle), and have two purposes: they admit air to the internal tissues, as it were for breathing, and they also emit water vapor. These lenticels are to be found on all trees, even where the bark is very thick, as old oaks and chestnuts, but in these the lenticels are in the bottoms of the deep cracks. There is a great difference in the inflammability of bark, some, like that of the big trees of California, Fig. 54, p. 209, which is often two feet thick, being practically incombustible, and hence serving to protect the tree; while some bark, as canoe birch, is laden with an oil which burns furiously. It therefore makes admirable kindling for camp fires, even in wet weather.

Inside the cork is the "phloem" or "bast," which, by the way, gives its name to the bass tree, the inner bark of which is very tough and fibrous and therefore used for mat and rope making. In a living tree, the bast fibers serve to conduct the nourishment which has been made in the leaves down thru the stem to the growing parts.

(2) The cambium. Inside of the rind and between it and the wood, there is, on living trees, a slimy coat called cambium (Med. Latin, exchange). This is the living, growing part of the stem, familiar to all who have peeled it as the sticky, slimy coat between the bark and the wood of a twig. This is what constitutes the fragrant, mucilaginous inner part of the bark of slippery elm. Cambium is a tissue of young and growing cells, in which the new cells are formed, the inner ones forming the wood and the outer ones the bark.

In order to understand the cambium and its function, consider its appearance in a bud, Fig. 5. A cross-section of the bud of a growing stem examined under the microscope, looks like a delicate mesh of thin membrane, filled in with a viscid semi-fluid substance which is called "protoplasm" (Greek, protos, first; plasma, form). These meshes were first called "cells" by Robert Hooke, in 1667, because of their resemblance to the chambers of a honeycomb. The walls of these "cells" are their most prominent feature and, when first studied, were supposed to be the essential part; but later the slimy, colorless substance which filled the cells was found to be the essential part. This slimy substance, called protoplasm, constitutes the primal stuff of all living things. The cell walls themselves are formed from it. These young cells, at the apex of a stem, are all alike, very small, filled with protoplasm, and as yet, unaltered. They form embryonic tissue, i.e. one which will change. One change to which an cell filled with protoplasm is liable is division into two, a new partition wall forming within it. This is the way plant cells increase.

E, epidermis, the single outside layer of cells.

C, cortex, the region outside of the bundles.

HB, hard bast, the black, irregular ring protecting the soft bast.

SB, soft bast, the light, crescent-shaped parts.

Ca, cambium, the line between the soft bast and the wood.

W, wood, segments showing pores.

MR, medullary rays, lines between the bundles connecting the pith and the cortex.

MS, medullary sheath, the dark, irregular ring just inside the bundles.

P, pith, the central mass of cells.]

In young plant cells, the whole cavity of the chamber is filled with protoplasm, but as the cells grow older and larger, the protoplasm develops into different parts, one part forming the cell wall and in many cases leaving cavities within the cell, which become filled with sap. The substance of the cell wall is called cellulose (cotton and flax fibers consist of almost pure cellulose). At first it has no definite structure, but as growth goes on, it may become thickened in layers, or gummy, or hardened into lignin (wood), according to the function to be performed. Where there are a group of similar cells performing the same functions, the group is called a tissue or, if large enough, a tissue system.

When cells are changed into new forms, or "differentiated," as it is called, they become permanent tissues. These permanent tissues of the tree trunk constitute the various parts which we have noticed, viz., the rind, the pith and the wood.

The essentially living part of the tree, it should be remembered, is the protoplasm: where there is protoplasm, there is life and growth. In the stems of the conifers and broad-leaved trees--sometimes together called exogens-- this protoplasm is to be found in the buds and in the cambium sheath, and these are the growing parts of the tree. If we followed up the sheath of cambium which envelopes a stem, into a terminal bud, we should find that it passed without break into the protoplasm of the bud.

In the cross-section of a young shoot, we might see around the central pith or medulla, a ring of wedge-shaped patches. These are really bundles of cells running longitudinally from the rudiments of leaves thru the stem to the roots. They are made of protoplasm and are called the "procambium strands," Fig. 6.

In the monocotyledons (endogens) these procambium strands change completely into wood and bast, and so losing all their protoplasmic cambium, become incapable of further growth. This is why palms can grow only lengthwise, or else by forming new fibers more densely in the central mass. But in the conifers and broad-leaved trees, the inner part of each strand becomes wood and the outer part bast (bark). Between these bundles, connecting the pith in the center with the cortex on the outside of the ring of bundles, are parts of the original pith tissue of the stem. They are the primary pith or medullary rays (Latin, medulla, pith). The number of medullary rays depends upon the number of the bundles; and their form, on the width of the bundles, so that they are often large and conspicuous, as in oak, or small and indeed invisible, as in some of the conifers. But they are present in all exogenous woods, and can readily be seen with the microscope. Stretching across these pith rays from the cambium layer in one procambium strand to that in the others, the cambium formation extends, making a complete cylindrical sheath from the bud downward over the whole stem. This is the cambium sheath and is the living, growing part of the stem from which is formed the wood on the inside and the rind (bark) on the outside.

In the first year the wood and the bast are formed directly by the growth and change of the inner and outer cells respectively of the procambium strand, and all such material is called "primary;" but in subsequent years all wood, pith rays, and bast, originate in the cambium, and these growths are called "secondary."

(3) The wood of most exogens is made up of two parts, a lighter part called the sap-wood or splint-wood or alburnum, and a darker part called the heart-wood or duramen, Fig. 7. Sap-wood is really immature heartwood. The difference in color between them is very marked in some woods, as in lignum vitae and black walnut, and very slight in others, as spruce and bass. Indeed, some species never form a distinct heart-wood, birch (Betula alba) being an example.

In a living tree, sap-wood and heart-wood perform primarily quite different functions. The sap-wood carries the water from the roots to the leaves, stores away starch at least in winter, and in other ways assists the life of the tree. The proportional amount of sapwood varies greatly, often, as in long-leaf pine, constituting 40 per cent. of the stem.

As the sap-wood grows older, its cells become choked so that the sap can no longer flow thru them. It loses its protoplasm and starch and becomes heartwood, in which all cells are dead and serve only the mechanical function of holding up the great weight of the tree and in resisting wind pressures. This is the reason why a tree may become decayed and hollow and yet be alive and bear fruit. In a tree that is actually dead the sap-wood rots first.

Chemical substances infiltrate into the cell walls of heart-wood and hence it has a darker color than the sap-wood. Persimmon turns black, walnut purplish brown, sumac yellow, oak light brown, tulip and poplar yellowish, redwood and cedar brownish red. Many woods, as mahogany and oak, darken under exposure, which shows that the substances producing the color are oxidizable and unstable. Wood dyes are obtained by boiling and distilling such woods as sumach, logwood, red sanders, and fustic. Many woods also acquire distinct odors, as camphor, sandalwood, cedar, cypress, pine and mahogany, indicating the presence of oil.

As a rule heart-wood is more valuable for timber, being harder, heavier, and drier than sap-wood. In woods like hickory and ash, however, which are used for purposes that require pliability, as in baskets, or elasticity as in handles of rakes and hoes, sap-wood is more valuable than heart-wood.

In a transverse section of a conifer, for example Douglas spruce, Fig. 8, the wood is seen to lie in concentric rings, the outer part of the ring being darker in color than the inner part. In reality each of these rings is a section of an irregular hollow cone, each cone enveloping its inner neighbor. Each cone ordinarily constitutes a year's growth, and therefore there is a greater number of them at the base of a tree than higher up. These cones vary greatly in thickness, or, looking at a cross-section, the rings vary in width; in general, those at the center being thicker than those toward the bark. Variations from year to year may also be noticed, showing that the tree was well nourished one year and poorly nourished another year. Rings, however, do not always indicate a year's growth. "False rings" are sometimes formed by a cessation in the growth due to drouth, fire or other accident, followed by renewed growth the same season.

In a radial section of a log, Fig. 8, these "rings" appear as a series of parallel lines and if one could examine a long enough log these lines would converge, as would the cut edges in a nest of cones, if they were cut up thru the center, as in Fig. 9.

In a tangential section, the lines appear as broad bands, and since almost no tree grows perfectly straight, these lines are wavy, and give the characteristic pleasing "grain" of wood. Fig. 27, p. 35. The annual rings can sometimes be discerned in the bark as well as in the wood, as in corks, which are made of the outer bark of the cork oak, a product of southern Europe and northern Africa. Fig. 10.

The growth of the wood of exogenous trees takes place thru the ability, already noted, of protoplasmic cells to divide. The cambium cells, which have very thin walls, are rectangular in shape, broader tangentially than radially, and tapering above and below to a chisel edge, Fig. 11. After they have grown somewhat radially, partition walls form across them in the longitudinal, tangential direction, so that in place of one initial cell, there are two daughter cells radially disposed. Each of these small cells grows and re-divides, as in Fig. 12. Finally the innermost cell ceases to divide, and uses its protoplasm to become thick and hard wood. In like manner the outermost cambium cell becomes bast, while the cells between them continue to grow and divide, and so the process goes on. In nearly all stems, there is much more abundant formation of wood than of bast cells. In other words, more cambium cells turn to wood than to bast.

In the spring when there is comparatively little light and heat, when the roots and leaves are inactive and feeble, and when the bark, split by winter, does not bind very tightly, the inner cambium cells produce radially wide wood cells with relatively thin walls. These constitute the spring wood. But in summer the jacket of bark binds tightly, there is plenty of heat and light, and the leaves and roots are very active, so that the cambium cells produce thicker walled cells, called summer wood. During the winter the trees rest, and no development takes place until spring, when the large thin-walled cells are formed again, making a sharp contrast with those formed at the end of the previous season.

It is only at the tips of the branches that the cambium cells grow much in length; so that if a nail were driven into a tree twenty years old at, say, four feet from the ground, it would still be four feet from the ground one hundred years later.

Looking once more at the cross-section, say, of spruce, the inner portion of each ring is lighter in color and softer in texture than the outer portion. On a radial or tangential section, one's finger nail can easily indent the inner portion of the ring, tho the outer dark part of the ring may be very hard. The inner, light, soft portion of the ring is the part that grows in the spring and early summer, and is called the "spring wood" while the part that grows later in the season is called "summer wood." As the summer wood is hard and heavy, it largely determines the strength and weight of the wood, so that as a rule, the greater the proportion of the summer growth, the better the wood. This can be controlled to some extent by proper forestry methods, as is done in European larch forests, by "underplanting" them with beech.

In a normal tree, the summer growth forms a greater proportion of the wood formed during the period of thriftiest growth, so that in neither youth nor old age, is there so great a proportion of summer wood as in middle age.

It will help to make clear the general structure of wood if one imagines the trunk of a tree to consist of a bundle of rubber tubes crushed together, so that they assume angular shapes and have no spaces between them. If the tubes are laid in concentric layers, first a layer which has thin walls, then successive layers having thicker and thicker walls, then suddenly a layer of thin-walled tubes and increasing again to thick-walled ones and so on, such an arrangement would represent the successive annual "rings" of conifers.

The medullary rays. While most of the elements in wood run longitudinally in the log, it is also to be noted that running at right angles to these and radially to the log, are other groups of cells called pith rays or medullary rays (Latin, medulla, which means pith). These are the large "silver flakes" to be seen in quartered oak, which give it its beautiful and distinctive grain, Fig. 32, p. 38. They appear as long, grayish lines on a cross-section, as broad, shining bands on the radial section, and as short, thick lines tapering at each end on the tangential section. In other words, they are like flat, rectangular plates standing on edge and radiating lengthwise from the center of the tree. They vary greatly in size in different woods. In sycamore they are very prominent, Fig. 13. In oak they are often several hundred cells wide (i.e., up and down in the tree). This may amount to an inch or two. They are often twenty cells thick, tapering to one cell at the edge. In oak very many are also small, even microscopic. But in the conifers and also in some of the broad-leaved trees, altho they can be discerned with the naked eye on a split radial surface, still they are all very small. In pine there are some 15,000 of them to a square inch of a tangential section. They are to be found in all exogens. In a cross-section, say of oak, Fig. 14, it can readily be seen that some pith rays begin at the center of the tree and some farther out. Those that start from the pith are formed the first year and are called primary pith rays, while those that begin in a subsequent year, starting at the cambium of that year, are called secondary rays.

The function of the pith rays is twofold. (1) They transfer formative material from one part of a stem to another, communicating with both wood and bark by means of the simple and bordered pits in them, and (2) they bind the trunk together from pith to bark. On the other hand their presence makes it easier for the wood to split radially.

The substance of which they are composed is "parenchyma" (Greek, beside, to pour), which also constitutes the pith, the rays forming a sort of connecting link between the first and last growth of the tree, as the cambium cells form new wood each year.

If a cambium cell is opposite to a pith ray, it divides crosswise (transversely) into eight or ten cells one above another, which stretch out radially, retaining their protoplasm, and so continue the pith ray. As the tree grows larger, new, or secondary medullary rays start from the cambium then active, so that every year new rays are formed both thinner and shorter than the primary rays, Fig. 14.

Now suppose that laid among the ordinary thin-walled tubes were quite large tubes, so that one could tell the "ring" not only by the thin walls but by the presence of large tubes. That would represent the ring-porous woods, and the large tubes would be called vessels, or tracheae. Suppose again that these large tubes were scattered in disorder thru the layers. This arrangement would represent the diffuse-porous woods.

By holding up to the light, thin cross-sections of spruce or pine, Fig. 15, oak or ash, Fig. 16, and bass or maple, Fig. 17, these three quite distinct arrangements in the structure may be distinguished. This fact has led to the classification of woods according to the presence and distribution of "pores," or as they are technically called, "vessels" or "tracheae." By this classification we have:

(1) Non-porous woods, which comprise the conifers, as pine and spruce.

(2) Ring-porous woods, in which the pores appear (in a cross-section) in concentric rings, as in chestnut, ash and elm.

(3) Diffuse-porous woods, in which (in a cross-section) the rings are scattered irregularly thru the wood, as in bass, maple and yellow poplar.

In order to fully understand the structure of wood, it is necessary to examine it still more closely thru the microscope, and since the three classes of wood, non-porous, ring-porous and diffuse-porous, differ considerably in their minute structure, it is well to consider them separately, taking the simplest first.

Non-porous woods. In examining thru the microscope a transverse section of white pine, Fig. 18:

(1) The most noticeable characteristic is the regularity of arrangement of the cells. They are roughly rectangular and arranged in ranks and files.

(2) Another noticeable feature is that they are arranged in belts, the thickness of their walls gradually increasing as the size of the cells diminishes. Then the large thin-walled cells suddenly begin again, and so on. The width of one of these belts is the amount of a single year's growth, the thin-walled cells being those that formed in spring, and the thick-walled ones those that formed in summer, the darker color of the summer wood as well as its greater strength being caused by there being more material in the same volume.

(3) Running radially (up and down in the picture) directly thru the annual belts or rings are to be seen what looks like fibers. These are the pith or medullary rays. They serve to transfer formative material from one part of the stem to another and to bind the tree together from pith to bark.

(4) Scattered here and there among the regular cells, are to be seen irregular gray or yellow dots which disturb the regularity of the arrangement. These are resin ducts. (See cross-section of white pine, Fig. 18.) They are not cells, but openings between cells, in which the resin, an excretion of the tree, accumulates, oozing out when the tree is injured. At least one function of resin is to protect the tree from attacks of fungi.

Looking now at the radial section, Fig. 18:

(5) The first thing to notice is the straightness of the long cells and their overlapping where they meet endwise, like the ends of two chisels laid together, Fig. 11.

(6) On the walls of the cells can be seen round spots called "pits." These are due to the fact that as the cell grows, the cell walls thicken, except in these small spots, where the walls remain thin and delicate. The pit in a cell wall always coincides with the pit in an adjoining cell, there being only a thin membrane between, so that there is practically free communication of fluids between the two cells. In a cross-section the pit appears as a canal, the length of which depends upon the thickness of the walls. In some cells, the thickening around the pits becomes elevated, forming a border, perforated in the center. Such pits are called bordered pits. These pits, both simple and bordered, are waterways between the different cells. They are helps in carrying the sap up the tree.

(7) The pith rays are also to be seen running across and interwoven in the other cells. It is to be noticed that they consist of several cells, one above another.

In the tangential section, Fig. 18:

(8) The straightness and overlapping of the cells is to be seen again, and

(9) The numerous ends of the pith rays appear.

In a word, the structure of coniferous wood is very regular and simple, consisting mainly of cells of one sort, the pith rays being comparatively unnoticeable. This uniformity is what makes the wood of conifers technically valuable.

The cells of conifers are called tracheids, meaning "like tracheae." They are cells in which the end walls persist, that is, are not absorbed and broken down when they meet end to end. In other words, conifers do not have continuous pores or vessels or "tracheae," and hence are called "non-porous" woods.

But in other woods, the ends of some cells which meet endwise are absorbed, thus forming a continuous series of elements which constitute an open tube. Such tubes are known as pores, or vessels, or "tracheae," and sometimes extend thru the whole stem. Besides this marked difference between the porous and non-porous woods, the porous woods are also distinguished by the fact that instead of being made up, like the conifers of cells of practically only one kind, namely tracheids, they are composed of several varieties of cells. Besides the tracheae and tracheids already noted are such cells as "wood fiber," "fibrous cells," and "parenchyma." Fig. 19. Wood fiber proper has much thickened lignified walls and no pits, and its main function is mechanical support. Fibrous cells are like the wood fibers except that they retain their protoplasm. Parenchyma is composed of vertical groups of short cells, the end ones of each group tapering to a point, and each group originates from the transverse division of one cambium cell. They are commonly grouped around the vessels (tracheae). Parenchyma constitutes the pith rays and other similar fibers, retains its protoplasm, and becomes filled with starch in autumn.

[Illustration: Fig. 19. Isolated Fibers and Cells. a, four cells of wood parenchyma; b, two cells from a pith ray; c, a single cell or joint of a vessel, the openings, x, x, leading into its upper and lower neighbors; d, tracheid; e, wood fiber proper. After Roth.]

The most common type of structure among the broad-leaved trees contains tracheae, trachaeids, woody fiber, fibrous cells and parenchyma. Examples are poplars, birch, walnut, linden and locust. In some, as ash, the tracheids are wanting; apple and maple have no woody fiber, and oak and plum no fibrous cells.

This recital is enough to show that the wood of the broad-leaved trees is much more complex in structure than that of the conifers. It is by means of the number and distribution of these elements that particular woods are identified microscopically. See p. 289.

Ring-porous woods. Looking thru the microscope at a cross-section of ash, a ring-porous wood, Fig. 20:

(1) The large round or oval pores or vessels grouped mostly in the spring wood first attract attention. Smaller ones, but still quite distinct, are to be seen scattered all thru the wood. It is by the number and distribution of these pores that the different oak woods are distinguished, those in white oak being smaller and more numerous, while in red oak they are fewer and larger. It is evident that the greater their share in the volume, the lighter in weight and the weaker will be the wood. In a magnified cross-section of some woods, as black locust, white elm and chestnut, see Chap. III, beautiful patterns are to be seen composed of these pores. It is because of the size of these pores and their great number that chestnut is so weak.

(2) The summer wood is also distinguishable by the fact that, as with the conifers, its cells are smaller and its cell walls thicker than those of the spring wood. The summer wood appears only as a narrow, dark line along the largest pores in each ring.

(3) The lines of the pith rays are very plain in some woods, as in oak. No. 47, Chap. III.

(4) The irregular arrangement and

(5) Complex structure are evident, and these are due to the fact that the wood substance consists of a number of different elements and not one (tracheids) as in the conifers.

Looking at the radial section, Fig. 20:

(6) If the piece is oak, the great size of the medullary rays is most noticeable. Fig. 32, p. 38. They are often an inch or more wide; that is, high, as they grow in the tree. In ash they are plain, seen thru the microscope, but are not

prominent.

(7) The interweaving of the different fibers and the variety of their forms show the structure as being very complex.

In the tangential section, Fig. 20:

(8) The pattern of the grain is seen to be marked not so much by the denseness of the summer wood as by the presence of the vessels (pores).

(9) The ends of the pith rays are also clear.

In diffuse porous woods, the main features to be noticed are: In the transverse section, Fig. 21:

(1) The irregularity with which the pores are scattered,

(2) The fine line of dense cells which mark the end of the year's growth,

(3) The radiating pith rays,

(4) The irregular arrangement and,

(5) The complex structure.

In the radial section, Fig. 21:

(6) The pith rays are evident. In sycamore, No. 53, Chap. III, they are quite large.

(7) The interweaving of the fibers is to be noted and also their variety.

In the tangential section, Fig. 21:

(8) The grain is to be traced only dimly, but the fibers are seen to run in waves around the pith rays.

(9) The pith rays, the ends of which are plainly visible.

THE GRAIN OF WOOD.

The term "grain" is used in a variety of meanings which is likely to cause confusion. This confusion may be avoided, at least in part, by distinguishing between grain and texture, using the word grain to refer to the arrangement or direction of the wood elements, and the word texture to refer to their size or quality, so far as these affect the structural character of the wood. Hence such qualifying adjectives as coarse and fine, even and uneven, straight and cross, including spiral, twisted, wavy, curly, mottled, bird's-eye, gnarly, etc., may all be applied to grain to give it definite meaning, while to texture the proper modifying adjectives are coarse and fine, even and uneven.

Usually the word grain means the pattern or "figure" formed by the distinction between the spring wood and the summer wood. If the annual rings are wide, the wood is, in common usage, called "coarse grained," if narrow, "fine grained," so that of two trees of the same species, one may be coarse grained and the other fine grained, depending solely on the accident of fast or slow growth.

The terms coarse grain and fine grain are also frequently used to distinguish such ring-porous woods as have large prominent pores, like chestnut and ash, from those having small or no pores, as cherry and lignum vitae. A better expression in this case would be coarse and fine textured. When such coarse textured woods are stained, the large pores in the spring wood absorb more stain than the smaller elements in the summer wood, and hence the former part appears darker. In the "fine grained" (or better, fine textured,) woods the pores are absent or are small and scattered, and the wood is hard, so that they are capable of taking a high polish. This indicates the meaning of the words coarse and fine in the mind of the cabinet-maker, the reference being primarily to texture.

If the elements of which a wood are composed are of approximately uniform size, it would be said to have a uniform texture, as in white pine, while uniform grain would mean, that the elements, tho of varying sizes, were evenly distributed, as in the diffuse-porous woods.

The term "grain" also refers to the regularity of the wood structure. An ideal tree would be composed of a succession of regular cones, but few trees are truly circular in cross-section and even in those that are circular, the pith is rarely in the center, showing that one side of the tree, usually the south side, is better nourished than the other, Fig. 14, p. 23.

The normal direction of the fibers of wood is parallel to the axis of the stem in which they grow. Such wood is called "straight-grained," Fig. 22, but there are many deviations from this rule. Whenever the grain of the wood in a board is, in whole or in part, oblique to the sides of the board, it is called "cross-grained." An illustration of this is a bend in the fibers, due to a bend in the whole tree or to the presence of a neighboring knot. This bend makes the board more difficult to plane. In many cases, probably in more cases than not, the wood fibers twist around the tree. (See some of the logs in Fig. 107, p. 254.) This produces "spiral" or "twisted" grain.

Often, as in mahogany and sweet gum, the fibers of several layers twist first in one direction and then those of the next few layers twist the other way, Fig. 24. Such wood is peculiarly cross-grained, and is of course hard to plane smooth. But when a piece is smoothly finished the changing reflection of light from the surface gives a beautiful appearance, which can be enhanced by staining and polishing. It constitutes the characteristic "grain" of striped mahogany, Fig. 23. It is rarely found in the inner part of the tree.

Sometimes the grain of wood is "cross," because it is "wavy" either in a radial or a tangential section, as in maple, Fig. 25, and Fig. 26.

"Curly grain" refers to the figure of circlets and islets and contours, often of great beauty, caused by cutting a flat surface in crooked-grained wood. See Fig. 27, curly long-leaf pine, and Fig. 28, yellow poplar. When such crookedness is fine and the fibers are contorted and, as it were, crowded out of place, as is common in and near the roots of trees, the effect is called "burl," Fig. 29. The term burl is also used to designate knots and knobs on tree trunks, Fig. 31. Burl is used chiefly in veneers.

Irregularity of grain is often caused by the presence of adventitious and dormant buds, which may be plainly seen as little knobs on the surface of some trees under the bark. In most trees, these irregularities are soon buried and smoothed over by the successive annual layers of wood, but in some woods there is a tendency to preserve the irregularities. On slash (tangent) boards of such wood, a great number of little circlets appear, giving a beautiful grain, as in "Bird's-eye maple," Fig. 30. These markings are found to predominate in the inner part of the tree. This is not at all a distinct variety of maple, as is sometimes supposed, but the common variety, in which the phenomenon frequently appears. Logs of great value, having bird's-eyes, have often unsuspectingly been chopped up for fire wood.

The term "grain" may also mean the "figure" formed by the presence of pith rays, as in oak, Fig. 32, or beech, or the word "grain" may refer simply to the uneven deposit of coloring matter as is common in sweet gum, Fig. 33, black ash, or Circassian walnut.

The presence of a limb constitutes a knot and makes great irregularity in the grain of wood, Fig. 34. In the first place, the fibers on the upper and lower sides of the limb behave differently, those on the lower side running uninterruptedly from the stem into the limb, while on the upper side the fibers bend aside making an imperfect connection. Consequently to split a knot it is always necessary to start the split from the lower side. On the other hand it is easier to split around a knot than thru it. The texture as well as the grain of wood is modified by the presence of a branch. The wood in and around a knot is much harder than the main body of the trunk on account of the crowding together of the elements. Knots are the remnants of branches left in the trunk. These once had all the parts of the trunk itself, namely bark, cambium, wood, and pith. Normally, branches grow from the pith, tho some trees, as Jack pine and redwood, among the conifers, and most of the broad-leaf trees have the power of putting out at any time adventitious buds which may develop into branches. When a branch dies, the annual layer of wood no longer grows upon it, but the successive layers of wood on the trunk itself close tighter and tighter around it, until it is broken off. Then, unless it has begun to decay, it is successively overgrown by annual layers, so that no sign of it appears until the trunk is cut open. A large trunk perfectly clean of branches on the outside may have many knots around its center, remnants of branches which grew there in its youth, as in Fig. 34, and Fig. 8, p. 18. The general effect of the presence of a knot is, that the fibers that grow around and over it are bent, and this, of course, produces crooked grain.

Following are the designations given to different knots by lumbermen: A sound knot is one which is solid across its face and is as hard as the wood surrounding it and fixed in position. A pin knot is sound, but not over 1/4" in diameter. A standard knot is sound, but not over 1-1/2" in diameter. A large knot is sound, and over 1-1/2" in diameter. A spike knot is one sawn in a lengthwise position. A dead, or, loose knot is one not firmly held in place by growth or position.

(4) Pith. At the center or axis of the tree is the pith or medulla, Fig. 34. In every bud, that is, at the apex of every stem and branch, the pith is the growing part; but as the stem lengthens and becomes overgrown by successive layers of wood the pith loses its vital function. It does not grow with the plant except at the buds. It varies in thickness, being very small,-- hardly more than 1/16", in cedar and larch,--and so small in oak as to be hardly discernible; and what there is of it turns hard and dark. In herbs and shoots it is relatively large, Fig. 5, p. 15, in a three-year old shoot of elder, for example, being as wide as the wood. In elder, moreover, it dies early and pulverizes, leaving the stem hollow. Its function is one of only temporary value to the plant.

THE STRUCTURE OF WOOD.

REFERENCES:[A]

Roth, Forest Bull. No. 10, pp. 11-23. Boulger, pp. 1-39. Sickles, pp. 11-20. Pinchot, Forest Bull. No. 24, I, pp. 11-24. Keeler, pp. 514-517. Curtis, pp. 62-85. Woodcraft, 15: 3, p. 90. Bitting, Wood Craft, 5: 76, 106, 144, 172, (June-Sept. 1906). Ward, pp. 1-38. Encyc. Brit., 11th Ed., "Plants," p. 741. Strasburger, pp. 120-144 and Part II, Sec. II. Snow, pp. 7-9, 183.

[Footnote A: For general bibliography, see p. 4.]

CHAPTER II.

PROPERTIES OF WOOD.

There are many properties of wood,--some predominant in one species, some in another,--that make it suitable for a great variety of uses. Sometimes it is a combination of properties that gives value to a wood. Among these properties are hygroscopicity, shrinkage, weight, strength, cleavability, elasticity, hardness, and toughness.

THE HYGROSCOPICITY[1] OF WOOD.

It is evident that water plays a large part in the economy of the tree. It occurs in wood in three different ways: In the sap which fills or partly fills the cavities of the wood cells, in the cell walls which it saturates, and in the live protoplasm, of which it constitutes 90 per cent. The younger the wood, the more water it contains, hence the sap-wood contains much more than the heart-wood, at times even twice as much.

In fresh sap-wood, 60 per cent. of the water is in the cell cavities, 35 per cent. in the cell walls, and only 5 per cent. in the protoplasm. There is so much water in green wood that a sappy pole will soon sink when set afloat. The reason why there is much less water in heart-wood is because its cells are dead and inactive, and hence without sap and without protoplasm. There is only what saturates the cell walls. Even so, there is considerable water in heart-wood.[2]

The lighter kinds have the most water in the sap-wood, thus sycamore has more than hickory.

Curiously enough, a tree contains about as much water in winter as in summer. The water is held there, it is supposed, by capillary attraction, since the cells are inactive, so that at all times the water in wood keeps the cell walls distended.

THE SHRINKAGE OF WOOD.

When a tree is cut down, its water at once begins to evaporate. This process is called "seasoning."[A] In drying, the free water within the cells keeps the cell walls saturated; but when all the free water has been removed, the cell walls begin to yield up their moisture. Water will not flow out of wood unless it is forced out by heat, as when green wood is put on a fire. Ordinarily it evaporates slowly.

[Footnote A: See Handwork in Wood, Chapter III.]

The water evaporates faster from some kinds of wood than from other kinds, e.g., from white pine than from oak, from small pieces than from large, and from end grain than from a longitudinal section; and it also evaporates faster in high than in low temperatures.

Evaporation affects wood in three respects, weight, strength, and size. The weight is reduced, the strength is increased, and shrinkage takes place. The reduction in weight and increase in strength, important as they are, are of less importance than the shrinkage, which often involves warping and other distortions. The water in wood affects its size by keeping the cell walls distended.

If all the cells of a piece of wood were the same size, and had walls the same thickness, and all ran in the same direction, then the shrinkage would be uniform. But, as we have seen, the structure of wood is not homogeneous. Some cellular elements are large, some small, some have thick walls, some thin walls, some run longitudinally and some (the pith rays) run radially. The effects will be various in differently shaped pieces of wood but they can easily be accounted for if one bears in mind these three facts: (1) that the shrinkage is in the cell wall, and therefore (2) that the thick-walled cells shrink more than thin-walled cells and (3) that the cells do not shrink much, if any, lengthwise.

(1) The shrinkage of wood takes place in the walls of the cells that compose it, that is, the cell walls become thinner, as indicated by the dotted lines in Fig. 35, which is a cross-section of a single cell. The diameter of the whole cell becomes less, and the opening, or lumen, of the cell becomes larger.

(2) Thick-walled cells shrink more than thin-walled cells, that is, summer cells more than spring cells. This is due to the fact that they contain more shrinkable substance. The thicker the wall, the more the shrinkage.

Consider the effects of these changes; ordinarily a log when drying begins to "check" at the end. This is to be explained thus: Inasmuch as evaporation takes place faster from a cross than from a longitudinal section, because at the cross-section all the cells are cut open, it is to be expected that the end of a piece of timber, Fig. 36, A, will shrink first. This would tend to make the end fibers bend toward the center of the piece as in B, Fig. 36. But the fibers are stiff and resist this bending with the result that the end splits or "checks" as in C, Fig. 36. But later, as the rest of the timber dries out and shrinks, it becomes of equal thickness again and the "checks" tend to close.

(3) For some reason, which has not been discovered, the cells or fibers of wood do not shrink in length to any appreciable extent. This is as true of the cells of pith rays, which run radially in the log, as of the ordinary cells, which run longitudinally in it.

In addition to "checking" at the end, logs ordinarily show the effect of shrinkage by splitting open radially, as in Fig. 37. This is to be explained by two factors, (1) the disposition of the pith (or medullary) rays, and (2) the arrangement of the wood in annual rings.

(1) The cells of the pith rays, as we have seen in Chapter I, run at right angles to the direction of the mass of wood fibers, and since they shrink according to the same laws that other cells do, viz., by the cell wall becoming thinner but not shorter, the strain of their shrinkage is contrary to that of the main cells. The pith rays, which consist of a number of cells one above the other, tend to shrink parallel to the length of the wood, and whatever little longitudinal shrinkage there is in a board is probably due mostly to the shrinkage of the pith rays. But because the cells of pith rays do not appreciably shrink in their length, this fact tends to prevent the main body of wood from shrinking radially, and the result is that wood shrinks less radially than tangentially. Tangentially is the only way left for it to shrink. The pith rays may be compared to the ribs of a folding fan, which keep the radius of unaltered length while permitting comparative freedom for circumferential contraction.

(2) It is evident that since summer wood shrinks more than spring wood, this fact will interfere with the even shrinkage of the log. Consider first the tangential shrinkage. If a section of a single annual ring of green wood of the shape A B C D, in Fig. 38, is dried and the mass shrinks according to the thickness of the cell walls, it will assume the shape A' B' C' D'. When a number of rings together shrink, the tangential shrinkage of the summer wood tends to contract the adjoining rings of spring wood more than they would naturally shrink of themselves. Since there is more of the summer-wood substance, the spring-wood must yield, and the log shrinks circumferentially. The radial

shrinkage of the summer-wood, however, is constantly interrupted by the alternate rows of spring-wood, so that there would not be so much radial as circumferential shrinkage. As a matter of fact, the tangential or circumferential shrinkage is twice as great as the radial shrinkage.

Putting these two factors together, namely, the lengthwise resistance of the pith rays to the radial shrinkage of the mass of other fibers, and second, the continuous bands of summer wood, comparatively free to shrink circumferentially, and the inevitable happens; the log splits. If the bark is left on and evaporation hindered, the splits will not open so wide.

There is still another effect of shrinkage. If, immediately after felling, a log is sawn in two lengthwise, the radial splitting may be largely avoided, but the flat sides will tend to become convex, as in Fig. 39. This is explained by the fact that circumferential shrinkage is greater than radial shrinkage.

If a log is "quartered,"[A] the quarters split still less, as the inevitable shrinkage takes place more easily. The quarters then tend to assume the shape shown in Fig. 40, C. If a log is sawed into timber, it checks from the center of the faces toward the pith, Fig. 40, D. Sometimes the whole amount of shrinkage may be collected in one large split. When a log is slash-sawed, Fig. 40, I, each board tends to warp so that the concave side is away from the center of the tree. If one plank includes the pith, Fig. 40, E and H, that board will become thinner at its edges than at its center, i.e., convex on both faces. Other forms assumed by wood in shrinking are shown in Fig. 40. In the cases A-F the explanation is the same; the circumferential shrinkage is more than the radial. In J and K the shapes are accounted for by the fact that wood shrinks very little longitudinally.

[Footnote A: See Handwork in Wood, p. 42.]

Warping is uneven shrinkage, one side of the board contracting more than the other. Whenever a slash board warps under ordinary conditions, the convex side is the one which was toward the center of the tree. However, a board may be made to warp artificially the other way by applying heat to the side of the board toward the center of the tree, and by keeping the other side moist. The board will warp only sidewise; lengthwise it remains straight unless the treatment is very severe. This shows again that water distends the cells laterally but not longitudinally.

The thinning of the cell walls due to evaporation, is thus seen to have three results, all included in the term "working," viz.: shrinkage, a diminution in size, splitting, due to the inability of parts to cohere under the strains to which they are subjected, and warping, or uneven shrinkage.

In order to neutralize warping as much as possible in broad board structures, it is common to joint the board with the annual rings of each alternate board curving in opposite directions, as shown in Handwork in Wood, Fig. 280, a, p. 188.

Under warping is included bowing. Bowing, that is, bending in the form of a bow, is, so to speak, longitudinal warping. It is largely due to crookedness or irregularity of grain, and is likely to occur in boards with large pith rays, as oak and sycamore. But even a straight-grained piece of wood, left standing on end or subjected to heat on one side and dampness on the other, will bow, as, for instance a board lying on the damp ground and in the sun.

Splitting takes various names, according to its form in the tree. "Check" is a term used for all sorts of cracks, and more particularly for a longitudinal crack in timber. "Shakes" are splits of various forms as: star shakes, Fig. 41, a, splits which radiate from the pith along the pith rays and widen outward; heart shakes, Fig. 41, b, splits crossing the central rings and widening toward the center; and cup or ring shakes, Fig. 41, c, splits between the annual rings. Honeycombing, Fig. 41, d, is splitting along the pith rays and is due largely to case hardening.

These are not all due to shrinkage in drying, but may occur in the growing tree from various harmful causes. See p. 232.

Wood that has once been dried may again be swelled to nearly if not fully its original size, by being soaked in water or subjected to wet steam. This fact is taken advantage of in wetting wooden wedges to split some kinds of soft stone. The processes of shrinking and swelling can be repeated indefinitely, and no temperature short of burning, completely prevents wood from shrinking and swelling.

Rapid drying of wood tends to "case harden" it, i.e., to dry and shrink the outer part before the inside has had a chance to do the same. This results in checking separately both the outside and the inside, hence special precautions need to be taken in the seasoning of wood to prevent this. When wood is once thoroly bent out of shape in shrinking, it is very difficult to straighten it again.

Woods vary considerably in the amounts of their shrinkage. The conifers with their regular structure shrink less and shrink more evenly than the broad-leaved woods.[3] Wood, even after it has been well seasoned, is subject to frequent changes in volume due to the varying amount of moisture in the atmosphere. This involves constant care in handling it and wisdom in its use. These matters are considered in Handwork in Wood, Chapter III, on the Seasoning of Wood.

THE WEIGHT OF WOOD.

Wood substance itself is heavier than water, as can readily be proved by immersing a very thin cross-section of pine in water. Since the cells are cut across, the water readily enters the cavities, and the wood being heavier than the water, sinks. In fact, it is the air enclosed in the cell cavities that ordinarily keeps wood afloat, just as it does a corked empty bottle, altho glass is heavier than water. A longitudinal shaving of pine will float longer than a cross shaving for the simple reason that it takes longer for the water to penetrate the cells, and a good sized white pine log would be years in getting water-soaked enough to sink. As long as a majority of the cells are filled with air it would float.

In any given piece of wood, then, the weight is determined by two factors, the amount of wood substance and the amount of water contained therein. The amount of wood substance is constant, but the amount of water contained is variable, and hence the weight varies accordingly. Moreover, considering the wood substance alone, the weight of wood substance of different kinds of wood is about the same; namely, 1.6 times as heavy as water, whether it is oak or pine, ebony or poplar. The reason why a given bulk of some woods is lighter than an equal bulk of others, is because there are more thin-walled and air-filled cells in the light woods. Many hard woods, as lignum vitae, are so heavy that they will not float at all. This is because the wall of the wood cells is very thick, and the lumina are small.

In order, then, to find out the comparative weights of different woods, that is, to see how much wood substance there is in a given volume of any wood, it is necessary to test absolutely dry specimens.

The weight of wood is indicated either as the weight per cubic foot or as specific gravity.

It is an interesting fact that different parts of the same tree have different weights, the wood at the base of the tree weighing more than that higher up, and the wood midway between the pith and bark weighing more than either the center or the outside.[4]

The weight of wood has a very important bearing upon its use. A mallet-head, for example, needs weight in a small volume, but it must also be tough to resist shocks, and elastic so as to impart its momentum gradually and not all at once, as an iron head does.

Weight is important, too, in objects of wood that are movable. The lighter the wood the better, if it is strong enough. That is why spruce is valuable for ladders; it is both light and strong. Chestnut would be a valuable wood for furniture if it were not weak, especially in the spring wood.

The weight of wood is one measure of its strength. Heavy wood is stronger than light wood of the same kind, for the simple reason that weight and strength are dependent upon the number and compactness of the fibers.[5]

THE STRENGTH OF WOOD.

Strength is a factor of prime importance in wood. By strength is meant the ability to resist stresses, either of tension (pulling), or of compression (pushing), or both together, cross stresses. When a horizontal timber is subjected to a downward cross stress, the lower half is under tension, the upper half is under compression and the line between is called the neutral axis, Fig. 42.

Wood is much stronger than is commonly supposed. A hickory bar will stand more strain under tension than a wrought iron bar of the same length and weight, and a block of long-leaf pine a greater compression endwise than a block of wrought iron of the same height and weight. It approaches the strength of cast iron under the same conditions.

Strength depends on two factors: the strength of the individual fibers, and the adhesive power of the fibers to each other. So, when a piece of wood is pulled apart, some of the fibers break and some are pulled out from among their neighbors. Under compression, however, the fibers seem to act quite independently of each other, each bending over like the strands of a rope when the ends are pushed together. As a consequence, we find that wood is far stronger under tension than under compression, varying from two to four times.

Woods do not vary nearly so much under compression as under tension, the straight-grained conifers, like larch and longleaf pine, being nearly as strong under compression as the hard woods, like hickory and elm, which have entangled fibers, whereas the hard woods are nearly twice as strong as the conifers under tension.

Moisture has more effect on the strength of wood than any other extrinsic condition. In sound wood under ordinary conditions, it outweighs all other causes which affect strength. When thoroly seasoned, wood is two or three times stronger, both under compression and in bending, than when green or water soaked.[6]

The tension or pulling strength of wood is much affected by the direction of the grain, a cross-grained piece being only 1/10th to 1/20th as strong as a straight-grained piece. But under compression there is not much difference; so that if a timber is to be subjected to cross strain, that is the lower half under tension and the upper half under compression, a knot or other cross-grained portion should be in the upper half.

[Illustration: Fig. 43. Shearing Strength is Measured by the Adhesion of the Portion A, B, C, D or to the Wood on both sides of it.]

Strength also includes the ability to resist shear. This is called "shearing strength." It is a measure of the adhesion of one part of the wood to an adjoining part. Shearing is what takes place when the portion of wood beyond a mortise near the end of a timber, A B C D, Fig. 43, is forced out by the tenon. In this case it would be shearing along the grain, sometimes called detrusion. The resistance of the portion A B C D, i.e., its power of adhesion to the wood adjacent to it on both sides, is its shearing strength. If the mortised piece were forced downward until it broke off the tenon at the shoulder, that would be shearing across the grain. The shearing resistance either with or across the grain is small compared with tension and compression. Green wood shears much more easily than dry, because moisture softens the wood and this reduces the adhesion of the fibers to each other.[7]

CLEAVABILITY OF WOOD.

Closely connected with shearing strength is cohesion, a property usually considered under the name of its opposite, cleavability, i.e., the ease of splitting.

When an ax is stuck into the end of a piece of wood, the wood splits in advance of the ax edge. See Handwork in Wood, Fig. 59, p. 52. The wood is not cut but pulled across the grain just as truly as if one edge were held and a weight were attached to the other edge and it were torn apart by tension. The length of the cleft ahead of the blade is determined by the elasticity of the wood. The longer the cleft, the easier to split. Elasticity helps splitting, and shearing strength and hardness hinder it.

A normal piece of wood splits easily along two surfaces, (1) along any radial plane, principally because of the presence of the pith rays, and, in regular grained wood like pine, because the cells are radially regular; and (2) along the annual rings, because the spring-wood separates easily from the next ring of summer-wood. Of the two, radial cleavage is 50 to 100 per cent. easier. Straight-grained wood is much easier to split than cross-grained wood in which the fibers are interlaced, and soft wood, provided it is elastic, splits easier than hard. Woods with sharp contrast between spring and summer wood, like yellow pine and chestnut, split very easily tangentially.

All these facts are important in relation to the use of nails. For instance, the reason why yellow pine is hard to nail and bass easy is because of their difference in cleavability.

ELASTICITY OF WOOD.

Elasticity is the ability of a substance when forced out of shape,--bent, twisted, compressed or stretched, to regain its former shape. When the elasticity of wood is spoken of, its ability to spring back from bending is usually meant. The opposite of elasticity is brittleness. Hickory is elastic, white pine is brittle.

Stiffness is the ability to resist bending, and hence is the opposite of pliability or flexibility. A wood may be both stiff and elastic; it may be even stiff and pliable, as ash, which may be made into splints for baskets and may also be used for oars. Willow sprouts are flexible when green, but quite brittle when dry.

Elasticity is of great importance in some uses of wood, as in long tool handles used in agricultural implements, such as rakes, hoes, scythes, and in axes, in archery bows, in golf sticks, etc., in all of which, hickory, our most elastic wood, is used.[8]

HARDNESS OF WOOD.

Hardness is the ability of wood to resist indentations, and depends primarily upon the thickness of the cell walls and the smallness of the cell cavities, or, in general, upon the density of the wood structure. Summer wood, as we have seen, is much harder than spring wood, hence it is important in using such wood as yellow pine on floors to use comb-grain boards, so as to present the softer spring wood in as narrow surfaces as possible. See Handwork in Wood, p. 41, and Fig. 55. In slash-grain boards, broad surfaces of both spring and summer wood appear. Maple which is uniformly hard makes the best floors, even better than oak, parts of which are comparatively soft.

The hardness of wood is of much consequence in gluing pieces together. Soft woods, like pine, can be glued easily, because the fibers can be forced close together. As a matter of fact, the joint when dry is stronger than the rest of the board. In gluing hard woods, however, it is necessary to scratch the surfaces to be glued in order to insure a strong joint. It is for the same reason that a joint made with liquid glue is safe on soft wood when it would be weak on hard wood.[9]

TOUGHNESS OF WOOD.

Toughness may be defined as the ability to resist sudden shocks and blows. This requires a combination of various qualities, strength, hardness, elasticity and pliability. The tough woods, par excellence, are hickory, rock elm and ash. They can be pounded, pulled, compressed and sheared. It is because of this quality that hickory is used for wheel spokes and for handles, elm for hubs, etc.

In the selection of wood for particular purposes, it is sometimes one, sometimes another, and more often still, a combination of qualities that makes it fit for use.[10]

It will be remembered that it was knowledge of the special values of different woods that made "the one horse shay," "The Deacon's Masterpiece."

"So the Deacon inquired of the village folk Where he could find the strongest oak, That couldn't be split nor bent nor broke,-- That was for spokes and floor and sills; He sent for lancewood to make the thills; The cross bars were ash, from the straightest trees, The panels of whitewood, that cuts like cheese, But lasts like iron for things like these. The hubs of logs from the "Settler's Ellum,"-- Last of its timber,--they couldn't sell 'em. Never an ax had seen their chips, And the wedges flew from between their lips, Their blunt ends frizzled like celery tips; Step and prop-iron, bolt and screw, Spring, tire, axle and linch pin too, Steel of the finest, bright and blue; Thorough brace, bison skin, thick and wide; Boot, top dasher from tough old hide, Found in the pit when the tanner died. That was the way to "put her through." 'There!' said the Deacon, 'naow she'll dew!'"

[Footnote 1: Hygroscopicity, "the property possessed by vegetable tissues of absorbing or discharging moisture and expanding or shrinking accordingly."-- Century Dictionary.]

[Footnote 2: This is shown by the following table, from Forestry Bulletin No. 10, p. 31, Timber, by Filibert Roth:

POUNDS OF WATER LOST IN DRYING 100 POUNDS OF GREEN WOOD IN THE KILN.

Sap-wood or Heart-wood outer part. or interior.

1. Pines, cedars, spruces, and firs 45-65 16-25 2. Cypress, extremely variable 50-65 18-60 3. Poplar, cottonwood, basswood 60-65 40-60 4. Oak, beech, ash, elm, maple, birch, hickory, chestnut, walnut, and sycamore 40-50 30-40]

[Footnote 3: The following table from Roth, p. 37, gives the approximate shrinkage of a board, or set of boards, 100 inches wide, drying in the open air:

Shrinkage Inches. 1. All light conifers (soft pine, spruce, cedar, cypress) 3

2. Heavy conifers (hard pine, tamarack, yew, honey locust, box elder, wood of old oaks) 4

3. Ash, elm, walnut, poplar, maple, beech, sycamore, cherry, black locust 5

4. Basswood, birch, chestnut, horse chestnut, blue beech, young locust 6

5. Hickory, young oak, especially red oak Up to 10

The figures are the average of radial and tangential shrinkages.]

[Footnote 4: How much different woods vary may be seen by the following table, taken from Filibert Roth, Timber, Forest Service Bulletin No. 10, p. 28:

WEIGHT OF KILN-DRIED WOOD OF DIFFERENT SPECIES.

--------------------------------+------------------------------- | Approximate. +------------+--------------------- | | Weight of | +---------+----------- | Specific | 1 cubic | 1,000 feet | weight. | foot. | of lumber. -------------------------------------+-----------+---------+----------- | | Pounds | Pounds (a) Very heavy woods: | | | Hickory, oak, persimmon, | | | osage, orange, black | | | locust, hackberry, blue | | | beech, best of elm, and ash | 0.70-0.80 | 42-48 | 3,700 (b) Heavy woods: | | | Ash, elm, cherry, birch, | | | maple, beech, walnut, sour | | | gum, coffee tree,

honey | | | locust, best of southern | | | pine, and tamarack | .60-.70 | 36-42
| 3,200 (c) Woods of medium weight: | | | Southern pine, pitch pine, | | |
tamarack, Douglas spruce, | | | western hemlock, sweet gum, | | | soft
maple, sycamore, light | | | sassafras, mulberry, | | | grades of birch and
cherry | .50-.60 | 30-36 | 2,700 (d) Light woods: | | | Norway and bull pine,
red | | | cedar, cypress, hemlock, | | | the heavier spruce and fir, | | |
redwood, basswood, chestnut, | | | butternut, tulip, catalpa, | | | buckeye,
heavier grades of | | | poplar | .40-.50 | 24-30 | 2,200 (e) Very light woods: |
| | White pine, spruce, fir, white | | | cedar, poplar | .30-.40 | 18-24 | 1,800 -
-----------------------------------+-----------+---------+-----------

[Footnote 5: For table of weights of different woods see Sargent, Jesup
Collection, pp. 153-157.]

[Footnote 6: See Forestry Bulletin No. 70, pp. 11, 12, and Forestry Circular
No. 108.]

[Footnote 7: For table of strengths of different woods, see Sargent, Jesup
Collection, pp. 166 ff.]

[Footnote 8: For table of elasticity of different woods, see Sargent, Jesup
Collection, pp. 163 ff.]

[Footnote 9: For table of hardnesses of different woods, see Sargent, Jesup
Collection, pp. 173 ff.]

[Footnote 10: For detailed characteristics of different woods see Chapter III.]

THE PROPERTIES OF WOOD.

REFERENCES[A]

Moisture and Shrinkage.

Roth, For. Bull., No. 10, pp. 25-37. Busbridge, Sci. Am. Sup. No. 1500. Oct. 1,
'04.

Weight, Strength, Cleavability, Elasticity and Toughness.

Roth, For. Bull., 10, p. 37-50. Boulger, pp. 89-108, 129-140. Roth, First Book, pp. 229-233. Sargent, Jesup Collection, pp. 153-176.

Forest Circulars Nos. 108 and 139.

[Footnote A: For general bibliography, see p. 4.]

CHAPTER III.

THE PRINCIPAL SPECIES OF AMERICAN WOODS.

NOTES.

The photographs of tangential and radial sections are life size. The microphotographs are of cross-sections and are enlarged 37-1/2 diameters.

Following the precedent of U. S. Forest Bulletin No. 17, Sudworth's Check List of the Forest Trees of the United States, the complicated rules for the capitalization of the names of species are abandoned and they are uniformly not capitalized.

On pages 192-195 will be found lists of the woods described, arranged in the order of their comparative weight, strength, elasticity, and hardness. These lists are based upon the figures in Sargent's The Jesup Collection.

In the appendix, p. 289, will be found a key for distinguishing the various kinds of wood.

Information as to current wholesale prices in the principal markets of the country can be had from the U. S. Dept. of Agriculture, The Forest Service, Washington, D. C., Record of Wholesale Prices of Lumber, List A. These lists are published periodically. No attempt is made in this book to give prices because: (1) only lists of wholesale prices are available; (2) the cuts and grades differ considerably, especially in soft woods (conifers); (3) prices are constantly varying; (4) the prices differ much in different localities.

WHITE PINE, WEYMOUTH PINE.

Named for Lord Weymouth, who cultivated it in England.

Pinus strobus Linnaeus.

Pinus, the classical Latin name; strobus refers to the cone, or strobile, from a Greek word, strobus, meaning twist.

HABITAT: (See map); now best in Michigan, Wisconsin and Minnesota.

CHARACTERISTICS OF THE TREE: Height, 100'-120', even 200'; diameter, 2'-4'; branches in whorls, cleans poorly; bark, dark gray, divided by deep longitudinal fissures into broad ridges; leaves in clusters of 5, 3"-5" long; cone drooping, 4"-10" long.

APPEARANCE OF WOOD: Color, heart-wood, very light brown, almost cream color, sap-wood, nearly white; non-porous; rings, fine but distinct; grain, straight; pith rays, very faint; resin ducts, small, inconspicuous.

PHYSICAL QUALITIES: Weight, very light (59th in this list); 27 lbs. per cu. ft.; sp. gr. 0.3854; strength, medium (55th in this list); elasticity, medium (47th in this list); soft (57th in this list); shrinkage 3 per cent.; warps very little; durability, moderate; works easily in every way; splits easily but nails well.

COMMON USES: Doors, window sashes and other carpentry, pattern-making, cabinet-work, matches.

REMARKS: This best of American woods is now rapidly becoming scarce and higher in price. Its uses are due to its uniform grain, on account of which it is easily worked and stands well. Known in the English market as yellow pine.

2

WESTERN WHITE PINE.

Pinus monticola Douglas.

Pinus, the classical Latin name; monticola means mountain-dweller.

[Illustration: Habitat.]

HABITAT: (See map); grows at great elevations, 7,000'-10,000'. Best in northern Idaho.

CHARACTERISTICS OF THE TREE: Height, 100'-160'; diameter, 4' to even 8'; branches, slender, spreading; bark, gray and brown, divided into squarish plates by deep longitudinal and cross fissures; leaves, 5 in sheath; cones, 12"x18" long.

APPEARANCE OF WOOD: Color, light brown or red, sap-wood nearly white; non-porous; rings, summer wood, thin and not conspicuous; grain, straight; rays, numerous, obscure; resin ducts, numerous and conspicuous tho not large.

PHYSICAL QUALITIES: Weight, very light (58th in this list); 24 lbs. per cu. ft.; sp. gr. 0.3908; strength, medium (56th in this list); elastic (35th in this list); soft (63d in this list); shrinkage, 3 per cent.; warps little; moderately durable; easy to work; splits readily but nails well.

COMMON USES: Lumber for construction and interior finish.

REMARKS: Closely resembles Pinus Strobus in appearance and quality of wood.

3

SUGAR PINE.

Sugar refers to sweetish exudation.

Pinus lambertiana Douglas.

Pinus, the classical Latin name; lambertiana, from the botanist, A. B. Lambert, whose chief work was on Pines.

HABITAT: (See map); grows on high elevations (5,000'), best in northern California.

CHARACTERISTICS OF THE TREE: Height, 100'-300'; diameter, 15"-20"; branches, in remote regular whorls; bark, rich purple or brown, thick, deep irregular fissures making long, flaky ridges; leaves, stout, rigid, in bundles of five; cones, 10"-18" long.

APPEARANCE OF WOOD: Color, pinkish brown, sap-wood, cream white; non-porous; rings, distinct; grain, straight; rays, numerous, obscure; resin ducts, numerous, large and conspicuous.

PHYSICAL QUALITIES: Weight, very light (61st in this list); 22 lbs. per cu. ft.; sp. gr. 0.3684; strength, weak (59th in this list); elasticity, medium (56th in this list); soft (53d in this list); shrinkage, 3 per cent.; warps little; durable; easily worked; splits little, nails well.

COMMON USES: Carpentry, interior finish, doors, blinds, shingles, barrels, etc.

REMARKS: Exudes a sweet substance from heart-wood. A magnificent and important lumber tree on Pacific coast.

4

NORWAY PINE. RED PINE.

Red refers to color of bark.

Pinus resinosa Solander.

Pinus, the classical Latin name; resinosa refers to very resinous wood.

HABITAT: (See map); grows best in northern Michigan, Wisconsin, and Minnesota.

CHARACTERISTICS OF THE TREE: Height, 70'-90'; diameter, 2'-3'; tall, straight;

branches in whorls, low; bark, thin, scaly, purplish and reddish-brown; longitudinal furrows, broad flat ridges; leaves, in twos in long sheaths; cones, 2".

APPEARANCE OF WOOD: Color of wood, pale red, sap-wood, wide, whitish; non-porous; rings summer wood broad, dark; grain, straight; rays, numerous, pronounced, thin; very resinous, but ducts small and few.

PHYSICAL QUALITIES: Weight, light, (43d in this list); 31 lbs. per cu. ft.; sp. gr. 0.4854; strong (39th in this list); elastic (16th in this list); soft (48th in this list); shrinkage, 3 per cent.; warps moderately; not durable; easy to work; splits readily, nails well.

COMMON USES: Piles, electric wire poles, masts, flooring.

REMARKS: Often sold with and as white pine. Resembles Scotch pine (Pinus sylvestris). Bark used to some extent for tanning. Grows in open groves.

5

WESTERN YELLOW PINE. BULL PINE.

Bull refers to great size of trunk.

Pinus ponderosa Lawson.

Pinus, the classical Latin name; ponderosa refers to great size of trunk.

HABITAT: (See map); best in Rocky Mountains.

CHARACTERISTICS OF THE TREE: Height, 100' to 300'; diameter, 6' to even 12'; branches, low, short trunk; bark, thick, dark brown, deep, meandering furrows, large, irregular plates, scaly; leaves, in twos or threes, 5" to 11" long; cones 3" to 6" long.

APPEARANCE OF WOOD: Color, light red, sap-wood, thick, nearly white, and very distinct; non-porous; rings, conspicuous; grain, straight; rays, numerous, obscure; very resinous but ducts small.

PHYSICAL QUALITIES: Weight, light (44th in this list); 25-30 lbs. per cu. ft.; sp. gr. 0.4715; strength, medium (45th in this list); elasticity, medium (41st in this list); hardness, medium (42nd in this list); shrinkage, 4 per cent.; warps ....; not durable; hard to work, brittle; splits easily in nailing.

COMMON USES: Lumber, railway ties, mine timbers.

REMARKS: Forms extensive open forests.

6

LONG-LEAF PINE. GEORGIA PINE.

Pinus palustris Miller.

Pinus, the classical Latin name; palustris means swampy, inappropriate here.

HABITAT: (See map); best in Louisiana and East Texas.

CHARACTERISTICS OF THE TREE: Height, 80'-100'; diameter, 2'-3'; trunk, straight, clean, branches high; bark, light brown, large, thin, irregular papery scales; leaves 8"-12" long, 3 in a sheath; cones 6"-10" long.

APPEARANCE OF WOOD: Heart-wood, spring wood light yellow, summer wood, red brown; sap wood, lighter; non-porous; rings, very plain and strongly marked; grain, straight; rays, numerous, conspicuous; very resinous, but resin ducts few and not large.

PHYSICAL QUALITIES: Heavy (18th in this list); 38 lbs. per cu. ft.; sp. gr. 0.6999; very strong (7th in this list); very elastic (4th in this list); hardness, medium (33d in this list); shrinkage, 4 per cent.; warps very little; quite durable; works hard, tough; splits badly in nailing.

COMMON USES: Joists, beams, bridge and building trusses, interior finish, ship building, and general construction work.

REMARKS: Almost exclusively the source of turpentine, tar, pitch and resin in the United States. Known in the English market as pitch pine.

7

SHORT-LEAF PINE. YELLOW PINE.

Pinus echinata Miller.

Pinus, the classical Latin name; echinata refers to spiny cones.

HABITAT: (See map); best in lower Mississippi basin.

CHARACTERISTICS OF THE TREE: Straight, tall trunk, sometimes 100' high; branches high; diameter 2'-4'; bark, pale grayish red-brown, fissures, running helter-skelter, making large irregular plates, covered with small scales; leaves in twos, 3" long; cones small.

APPEARANCE OF WOOD: Color, heartwood, summer wood, red, spring-wood, yellow; sap-wood, lighter; non-porous; annual rings very plain, sharp contrast between spring and summer wood; grain, straight, coarse; rays, numerous, conspicuous; very resinous, ducts large and many.

PHYSICAL QUALITIES: Weight, medium (32nd in this list); 32 lbs. per cu. ft.; sp. gr., 0.6104; very strong (18th in this list); very elastic (8th in this list); soft (38th in this list); shrinkage, 4 per cent.; warps little; durable; troublesome to work; likely to split along annual rings in nailing.

COMMON USES: Heavy construction, railroad ties, house trim, ship building, cars, docks, bridges.

REMARKS: Wood hardly distinguishable from long-leaf pine. Often forms pure forests. The most desirable yellow pine, much less resinous and more easily worked than others.

8

LOBLOLLY PINE. OLD FIELD PINE.

Loblolly may refer to the inferiority of the wood; old field refers to habit of spontaneous growth on old fields.

Pinus taeda Linnaeus.

Pinus, the classical Latin name; taeda, the classical Latin name for pitch-pine, which was used for torches.

HABITAT: (See map); grows best in eastern Virginia, and eastern North Carolina.

CHARACTERISTICS OF THE TREE: Height, 100'-150'; diameter, often 4'-5'; branches high; bark, purplish brown, shallow, meandering fissures, broad, flat, scaly ridges; leaves, 3 in sheath, 4"-7" long; cones 3"-5" long.

APPEARANCE OF WOOD: Color, heart-wood orange, sap-wood lighter; non-porous; rings very plain, sharp contrast between spring wood and summer wood; grain, straight, coarse; rays conspicuous; very resinous, but ducts few and small.

PHYSICAL QUALITIES: Weight, medium (39th in this list); 33 lbs. per cu. ft.; sp. gr. 0.5441; strong (26th in this list); elastic (17th in this list); medium hard (43d in this list); shrinkage, 4 per cent.; warps little; not durable; difficult to work, brittle; splits along rings in nailing.

COMMON USES: Heavy construction, beams, ship building, docks, bridges, flooring, house trim.

REMARKS: Resembles Long-leaf Pine, and often sold as such. Rarely makes pure forests.

9

SLASH PINE. CUBAN PINE.

Pinus caribaea Morelet. Pinus heterophylla (Ell.) Sudworth.

Pinus, the classical Latin name; caribaea refers to the Caribbean Islands;

heterophylla refers to two kinds of leaves.

HABITAT: (See map); grows best in Alabama, Mississippi, and Louisiana.

CHARACTERISTICS OF THE TREE: Height, sometimes 110', straight, tall, branching high; diameter 1'-3'; bark, dark red and brown, shallow irregular fissures; leaves, 2 or 3 in a sheath, 8"-12" long; cones, 4"-5" long.

APPEARANCE OF WOOD: Color, dark orange, sapwood lighter; non-porous; annual rings, plain, sharp contrast between spring wood and summer wood; grain, straight; rays numerous, rather prominent; very resinous, but ducts few.

PHYSICAL QUALITIES: Heavy (7th in this list); 39 lbs. per cu. ft.; sp. gr. 0.7504; very strong (6th in this list); very elastic (3d in this list); hard (24th in this list); shrinkage, 4 per cent.; warps little; quite durable; troublesome to work; splits along annual rings in nailing.

COMMON USES: Heavy construction, ship building, railroad ties, docks, bridges, house trim.

REMARKS: Similar to and often sold as Long-leaf Pine.

10

TAMARACK. LARCH. HACKMATACK.

Larix laricina (Du Roi) Koch. Larix americana Michaux.

Larix, the classical Latin name.

HABITAT: (See map); prefers swamps, "Tamarack swamps."

CHARACTERISTICS OF THE TREE: Height, 50'-60' and even 90', diameter 1'-3'; intolerant; tall, slender trunk; bark, cinnamon brown, no ridges, breaking into flakes; leaves, deciduous, pea-green, in tufts; cone, 1/2"-3/4", bright brown.

APPEARANCE OF WOOD: Color, light brown, sapwood hardly distinguishable; non-porous; rings, summer wood, thin but distinct, dark colored; grain, straight, coarse; rays, numerous, hardly distinguishable; very resinous, but ducts few and small.

PHYSICAL QUALITIES: Weight, medium (29th in this list); 39 lbs. per cu. ft.; sp. gr. 0.6236; strong (24th in this list); elastic (11th in this list); medium hard (40th in this list); shrinkage, 3 per cent.; warps ....; very durable; easy to work; splits easily.

COMMON USES: Ship building, electric wire poles, and railroad ties; used for boat ribs because of its naturally crooked knees; slenderness prevents common use as lumber.

REMARKS: Tree desolate looking in winter.

11

WESTERN LARCH. TAMARACK.

Larix occidentalis Nuttall.

Larix, the classical Latin name; occidentalis means western.

HABITAT: (See map); best in northern Montana and Idaho, on high elevations.

CHARACTERISTICS OF THE TREE: Height, 90'-130', even 250'; diameter 6'-8'; tall, slender, naked trunk, with branches high; bark, cinnamon red or purplish, often 12" thick, breaking into irregular plates, often 2' long; leaves, in tufts; deciduous; cones small.

APPEARANCE OF WOOD: Color, light red, thin, whitish, sap-wood; non-porous; grain, straight, fine; rays numerous, thin; very resinous, but ducts small and obscure.

PHYSICAL QUALITIES: Weight, heavy (11th in this list); 46 lbs. per cu. ft.; sp. gr. 0.7407; very strong (3d in this list); very elastic (1st in this list); medium hard (35th in this list); shrinkage, 4 per cent.; warps ....; very durable; rather hard to work, takes fine polish; splits with difficulty.

COMMON USES: Posts, railroad ties, fencing, cabinet material and fuel.

REMARKS: A valuable tree in the Northwest.

12

WHITE SPRUCE.

Picea canadensis (Miller) B. S. P. Picea alba Link.

Picea, the classical Latin name; white and alba refers to the pale color of the leaves, especially when young, and to the whitish bark.

HABITAT: (See map).

CHARACTERISTICS OF THE TREE: Height, 60'-100' and even 150'; diameter, 1'-2' and even 4'; long, thick branches; bark, light grayish brown, separating into thin plate-like scales, rather smooth appearance, resin from cuts forms white gum; leaves, set thickly on all sides of branch, finer than red spruce, odor disagreeable; cones, 2" long, cylindrical, slender, fall during second summer.

APPEARANCE OF WOOD: Color, light yellow, sap-wood, hardly distinguishable; non-porous; rings, wide, summer wood thin, not conspicuous; grain, straight; rays, numerous, prominent; resin ducts, few and minute.

PHYSICAL QUALITIES: Weight, light (51st in this list); 25 lbs. per cu. ft.; sp. gr., 0.4051; medium strong (42d in this list); elastic (29th in this list); soft (58th in this list); shrinks 3 per cent.; warps ....; fairly durable; easy to work, satiny surface; splits readily.

COMMON USES: Lumber and paper pulp; (not distinguished from Red and Black Spruce in market).

REMARKS: Wood very resonant, hence used for sounding boards. The most important lumber tree of the sub-arctic forest of British Columbia.

13

RED SPRUCE.[A]

Picea rubens Sargent.

Picea, the classical Latin name for the pitch pine; rubens refers to reddish bark, and perhaps to the reddish streaks in the wood.

HABITAT: (See map); stunted in north.

CHARACTERISTICS OF THE TREE: Height, 70'-80', even 100'; diameter, 2'-3', grows slowly; trunk, straight, columnar, branches in whorls, cleans well in forest; bark, reddish brown with thin irregular scales; leaves, needle-shaped, four-sided, pointing everywhere; cones, 1-1/4"-2" long, pendent, fall during the first winter.

APPEARANCE OF WOOD: Color, dull white with occasional reddish streaks; sap-wood not distinct; non-porous; rings, summer rings thin, but clearly defined; grain, straight; rays, faintly discernible; resin ducts, few and small.

PHYSICAL QUALITIES: Weight, light (47th in this list); 28 lbs. per cu. ft.; sp. gr., 0.4584; medium strong (41st in this list); elastic (21st in this list); soft (54th in this list); shrinkage, 3 per cent.; warps little; not durable; easy to plane, tolerably easy to saw, hard to chisel neatly; splits easily in nailing.

COMMON USES: Sounding boards, construction, paper pulp, ladders.

REMARKS: The exudations from this species are used as chewing gum. Bark of twigs is used in the domestic manufacture of beer. The use of the wood for sounding boards is due to its resonance, and for ladders to its strength and lightness.

[Footnote A: Not distinguished in the Jesup collection from Picea nigra.]

14

BLACK SPRUCE.[A]

Picea mariana (Miller) B. S. P. Picea nigra Link.

Picea, the classical Latin name for the pitch pine; mariana named for Queen Mary; black and nigra refer to dark foliage.

HABITAT: (See map); best in Canada.

CHARACTERISTICS OF THE TREE: Height, 50'-80' and even 100'; diameter, 6"-1' even 2'; branches, whorled, pendulous with upward curve; bark, gray, loosely attached flakes; leaves, pale blue-green, spirally set, pointing in all directions; cones, small, ovate-oblong, persistent for many years.

APPEARANCE OF WOOD: Color, pale, reddish, sap-wood, thin, white, not very distinct; non-porous; rings, summer wood, small thin cells; grain, straight; rays, few, conspicuous; resin ducts, few and minute.

PHYSICAL QUALITIES: Weight, light (47th in this list); 33 lbs. per cu. ft.; sp. gr., 0.4584; medium strong (41st in this list); elastic (21st in this list); soft (54th in this list); shrinkage, 3 per cent.; warps little; not durable; easy to work; splits easily in nailing.

COMMON USES: Sounding boards, lumber in Manitoba.

REMARKS: Not distinguished from Red Spruce commercially.

[Footnote A: Not distinguished in Jesup Collection from Picea rubens.]

15

WHITE SPRUCE. ENGELMANN'S SPRUCE.

Picea engelmanni (Parry) Engelmann.

Named for George Engelmann, an American botanist.

HABITAT: (See map); grows at very high elevations, forming forest at 8,000'-10,000'; best in British Columbia.

CHARACTERISTICS OF THE TREE: Height, 75'-100', even 150'; diameter, 2'-3', even 5'; branches whorled, spreading; bark, deeply furrowed, red-brown to purplish brown, thin, large, loose scales; leaves, blue-green, point in all directions; cones, 2" long, oblong, cylindrical.

APPEARANCE OF WOOD: Color, pale yellow or reddish, sap-wood hardly distinguishable; non-porous; rings, very fine, summer wood, narrow, not conspicuous; grain, straight, close; rays, numerous, conspicuous; resin ducts, small and few.

PHYSICAL QUALITIES: Weight, very light (57th in this list); 22 lbs. per cu. ft.; sp. gr. 0.3449; weak (61st in this list); elasticity medium (55th in this list); soft (56th in this list); shrinkage, 3 per cent.; warps ....; durable; easy to work; splits easily.

COMMON USES: Lumber.

REMARKS: A valuable lumber tree in the Rocky Mountains and the Cascades. Bark used for tanning.

16

TIDELAND SPRUCE. SITKA SPRUCE.

Picea sitchensis (Bongard) Carriere.

Picea, the classical Latin name for the pitch pine. Tideland refers to its habit of growth along the sea coast; sitchensis, named for Sitka.

HABITAT: (See map); best on Pacific slope of British Columbia and northwestern United States.

CHARACTERISTICS OF THE TREE: Height, 100'-150' and even 200' high; diameter 3'-4' and even 15'; trunk base enlarged; bark, thick, red-brown, scaly; leaves, standing out in all directions; cones, 2-1/2"-4" long, pendent, cylindrical, oval.

APPEARANCE OF WOOD: Color, light brown, sap-wood whitish; non-porous; rings, wide, summer wood, thin but very distinct, spring wood, not plain; grain, straight, coarse; rays, numerous, rather prominent; resin ducts, few and small.

PHYSICAL QUALITIES: Weight, light (52d in this list); 27 lbs. per cu. ft.; sp. gr. 0.4287; medium strong (53d in this list); elastic (31st in this list); soft (59th in this list); shrinkage, 3 per cent.; warps ....; durable; easy to work; splits easily.

COMMON USES: Interior finish, boat building and cooperage.

REMARKS: Largest of the spruces. Common in the coast belt forest.

17

HEMLOCK.

Tsuga canadensis (Linnaeus) Carriere.

Tsuga, the Japanese name latinized; canadensis named for Canada.

HABITAT: (See map); best in North Carolina and Tennessee.

CHARACTERISTICS OF THE TREE: Height, 60'-70', sometimes 100'; diameter, 2'-3'; branches, persistent, making trunk not very clean; bark, red-gray, narrow, rounded ridges, deeply and irregularly fissured; leaves, spirally arranged, but appear two-ranked; cones, 3/4" long, graceful.

APPEARANCE OF WOOD: Color, reddish brown, sap-wood just distinguishable; non-porous; rings, rather broad, conspicuous; grain, crooked; rays, numerous, thin; non-resinous.

PHYSICAL QUALITIES: Weight, light (53d in this list); 26 lbs. per cu. ft.; sp. gr. 0.4239; medium strong (44th in this list); elasticity, medium (40th in this list); soft (51st in this list); shrinkage, 3 per cent.; warps and checks badly; not durable; difficult to work, splintery, brittle; splits easily, holds nails well.

COMMON USES: Coarse, cheap lumber, as joists, rafters, plank walks and laths.

REMARKS: The poorest lumber. Bark chief source of tanning material.

18

WESTERN HEMLOCK. BLACK HEMLOCK.

Tsuga heterophylla (Rafinesque) Sargent.

Tsuga, the Japanese name latinized; heterophylla refers to two kinds of leaves.

HABITAT: (See map); best on coast of Washington and Oregon.

CHARACTERISTICS OF THE TREE: Height, 150'-200'; diameter, 6'-10'; branches, pendent, slender; bark, reddish gray, deep, longitudinal fissures between, broad, oblique, flat ridges; leaves, dark green, two-ranked; cones, small, like Eastern Hemlock.

APPEARANCE OF WOOD: Color, pale brown, sap-wood thin, whitish; non-porous; rings, narrow, summer wood thin but distinct; grain, straight, close; rays, numerous, prominent; non-resinous.

PHYSICAL QUALITIES: Light in weight, strong, elastic, hard;[A] shrinkage, 3 per cent.; warps ....; durable, more so than other American hemlocks; easier to work than eastern variety; splits badly.

COMMON USES: Lumber for construction.

REMARKS: Coming to be recognized as a valuable lumber tree.

19

DOUGLAS SPRUCE. OREGON PINE. RED FIR. DOUGLAS FIR.

Pseudotsuga mucronata (Rafinesque) Sudworth.

Pseudotsuga taxifolia (Lambert) Britton.

Pseudotsuga means false hemlock; mucronata refers to abrupt short point of leaf; taxifolia means yew leaf.

HABITAT: (See map); best in Puget Sound region.

CHARACTERISTICS OF THE TREE: Height, 175'-300'; diameter, 3'-5', sometimes 10'; branches high, leaving clean trunk; bark, rough, gray, great broad-rounded ridges, often appears braided; leaves, radiating from stem; cones, 2"-4" long.

APPEARANCE OF WOOD: Color, light red to yellow, sap-wood white; non-porous; rings, dark colored, conspicuous, very pronounced summer wood; grain, straight, coarse; rays, numerous, obscure; resinous.

PHYSICAL QUALITIES: Weight, medium (41st in this list); 32 lbs. per cu. ft, sp. gr. 0.5157; strong (21st in this list); very elastic (10th in this list); medium hard (45th in this list); shrinkage, 3 per cent. or 4 per cent.;, warps ....; durable; difficult to work, flinty, splits readily.

COMMON USES: Heavy construction, masts, flag poles, piles, railway ties.

REMARKS: One of the greatest and the most valuable of the western timber trees. Forms extensive forests.

20

GRAND FIR. WHITE FIR. LOWLAND FIR. SILVER FIR.

Abies grandis Lindley.

Abies, the classical Latin name.

HABITAT: (See map); best in Puget Sound region.

CHARACTERISTICS OF THE TREE: Height, in interior 100'; diameter, 2'; on coast, 250'-300' high; diameter, 2'-5'; long pendulous branches; bark, quite gray or gray brown, shallow fissures, flat ridges; leaves, shiny green above, silvery below, 1-1/2"-2" long, roughly two-ranked; cones, cylindrical, 2"-4" long.

APPEARANCE OF WOOD: Color, light brown, sap-wood lighter; non-porous; rings, summer cells broader than in other American species, dark colored, conspicuous; grain straight, coarse; rays, numerous, obscure; resinous.

PHYSICAL QUALITIES: Very light (62d in this list); 22 lbs. per cu. ft.; sp. gr., 0.3545; weak (62d in this list); elastic (34th in this list); soft (65th in this list); shrinkage, 3 per cent.; warps little; not durable; works easily; splits readily.

COMMON USES: Lumber and packing cases.

REMARKS: No resin ducts. Not a very valuable wood.

21

BIG TREE. SEQUOIA. GIANT SEQUOIA.

Sequoia washingtoniana (Winslow) Sudworth. Sequoia gigantea, Decaisne.

Sequoia latinized from Sequoiah, a Cherokee Indian; washingtoniana, in honor of George Washington.

HABITAT: (See map); in ten groves in southern California, at high elevation.

CHARACTERISTICS OF THE TREE: Height, 275', sometimes 320'; diameter, 20', sometimes 35'; trunk, swollen and often buttressed at base, ridged, often clear for 150'; thick horizontal branches; bark, 1'-2' thick, in great ridges, separates into loose, fibrous, cinnamon red scales, almost non-combustible; leaves, very small, growing close to stem; cones, 2"-3" long.

APPEARANCE OF WOOD: Color, red, turning dark on exposure, sap-wood thin, whitish; non-porous; rings, very plain; grain straight, coarse; rays, numerous, thin; non-resinous.

PHYSICAL QUALITIES: Light (65th in this list); 18 lbs. per cu. ft.; sp. gr., 0.2882; weak (63d in this list); brittle (62d in this list); very soft (61st in this list); shrinks little; warps little; remarkably durable; easy to work, splits readily, takes nails well.

COMMON USES: Construction, lumber, coffins, shingles.

REMARKS: Dimensions and age are unequalled; Big Tree and Redwood survivors of a prehistoric genus, once widely distributed. Some specimens 3600 years old.

22

REDWOOD. COAST REDWOOD. SEQUOIA.

Sequoia sempervirens (Lambert) Endlicher.

Sequoia, latinized from Sequoiah, a Cherokee Indian; sempervirens means ever living.

HABITAT: (See map); best in southern Oregon and northern California, near coast.

CHARACTERISTICS OF THE TREE: Height, 200'-340'; diameter, 10'-15', rarely 25'; clean trunk, much buttressed and swollen at base, somewhat fluted, branches very high; bark, very thick, 6"-12", rounded ridges, dark scales falling reveal inner red bark; leaves, small, two-ranked; cones, small, 1" long.

APPEARANCE OF WOOD: Color, red, turning to brown on seasoning, sapwood whitish; non-porous; rings, distinct; grain, straight; rays, numerous, very obscure; non-resinous.

PHYSICAL QUALITIES: Light in weight (55th in this list); 26 lbs. per cu. ft.; sp. gr. 0.4208; weak (58th in this list); brittle (60th in this list); soft (55th in this list); shrinks little; warps little; very durable; easily worked; splits readily; takes nails well.

COMMON USES: Shingles, construction, timber, fence posts, coffins, railway ties, water pipes, curly specimens used in cabinet work.

REMARKS: Low branches rare. Burns with difficulty. Chief construction wood of Pacific Coast. Use determined largely by durability.

23

BALD CYPRESS.

Bald refers to leaflessness of tree in winter.

Taxodium distichum (Linnaeus) L. C. Richard.

Taxodium means yew-like; distichum refers to the two-ranked leaves.

HABITAT: (See map); best in South Atlantic and Gulf States.

CHARACTERISTICS OF THE TREE: Height, 75', occasionally 150'; diameter, 4'-5'; roots project upward into peculiar knees; trunk strongly buttressed at base, straight, majestic and tapering; bark, light red, shallow fissures, flat plates, peeling into fibrous strips; leaves, long, thin, two-ranked, deciduous; cones, nearly globular, 1" in diameter.

APPEARANCE OF WOOD: Color, heart-wood, reddish brown, sap-wood, nearly white; non-porous; rings, fine and well marked; grain, nearly straight, burl is beautifully figured; rays, very obscure; non-resinous.

PHYSICAL QUALITIES: Light in weight (48th in this list); 29 lbs. per cu. ft.; sp. gr. 0.4543; medium strong (48th in this list); elastic (28th in this list); soft (52d in this list); shrinkage, 3 per cent.; warps but little, likely to check; very durable; easy to work, in splitting, crumbles or breaks; nails well.

COMMON USES: Shingles, posts, interior finish, cooperage, railroad ties, boats, and various construction work, especially conservatories.

REMARKS: Forms forests in swamps; subject to a fungous disease, making wood "peggy" or "pecky"; use largely determined by its durability. In New Orleans 90,000 fresh water cisterns are said to be made of it.

24

WESTERN RED CEDAR. CANOE CEDAR. GIANT ARBORVITAE.

Thuja plicata D. Don. Thuya gigantea Nuttall.

Thuya or Thuja, the classical Greek name; plicata refers to the folded leaves; gigantea refers to the gigantic size of the tree.

HABITAT: (See map); best in Puget Sound region.

CHARACTERISTICS OF THE TREE: Height, 100'-200'; diameter, 2'-10', even 15'; trunk has immense buttresses, often 16' in diameter, then tapers; branches, horizontal, short, making a dense conical tree; bark, bright cinnamon red, shallow fissures, broad ridges, peeling into long, narrow, stringy scales; leaves, very small, overlapping in 4 ranks, on older twigs, sharper and more remote; cones, 1/2" long, small, erect.

APPEARANCE OF WOOD: Color, dull brown or red, thin sap-wood nearly white; non-porous; rings, summer bands thin, dark colored, distinct; grain, straight, rather coarse; rays, numerous, obscure; non-resinous.

PHYSICAL QUALITIES: Very light in weight (60th in this list); medium strong (40th in this list); elastic (26th in this list); soft (60th in this list); shrinkage, 3 per cent.; warps and checks little; very durable; easy to work; splits easily.

COMMON USES: Interior finish, cabinet making, cooperage, shingles, electric wire poles.

REMARKS: Wood used by Indians for war canoes, totems and planks for lodges; inner bark used for ropes and textiles.

25

WHITE CEDAR.

Chamaecyparis thyoides (Linnaeus) B. S. P.

Chamaecyparis means low cypress; thyoides means like thuya (Aborvitae).

[Illustration: Habitat.]HABITAT: (See map); best in Virginia and North Carolina.

CHARACTERISTICS OF THE TREE: Height, 60'-80'; diameter, 2'-4'; branches, low, often forming impenetrable thickets; bark, light reddish brown, many fine longitudinal fissures, often spirally twisted around stem; leaves, scale-like, four-ranked; cones, globular, 1/4" diameter.

APPEARANCE OF WOOD: Color, pink to brown, sap-wood lighter; non-porous; rings, sharp and distinct; grain, straight; rays, numerous, obscure; non-resinous.

PHYSICAL QUALITIES: Very light in weight (64th in this list); 23 lbs. per cu. ft.; sp. gr. 0.3322); weak (64th in this list); brittle (63d in this list; soft (62d in this list); shrinkage 3 per cent.; warps little; extremely durable; easily worked; splits easily; nails well.

COMMON USES: Boats, shingles, posts, railway ties, cooperage.

REMARKS: Grows chiefly in swamps, often in dense pure forests. Uses determined largely by its durability.

26

LAWSON CYPRESS. PORT ORFORD CEDAR. OREGON CEDAR. WHITE CEDAR.

Chamaecyparis lawsoniana (A. Murray) Parlatore.

Chamaecyparis means low cypress.

HABITAT: (See map); best on coast of Oregon.

CHARACTERISTICS OF THE TREE: Height, 100'-200'; diameter, 4'-8', even 12'; base of trunk abruptly enlarged; bark, very thick, even 10" at base of trunk, inner and outer layers distinct, very deep fissures, rounded ridges; leaves, very small, 1/16" long, four-ranked, overlapped, flat sprays; cones, small, 1/4", globular.

APPEARANCE OF WOOD: Color, pinkish brown, sap-wood hardly distinguishable; non-porous; rings, summer wood thin, not conspicuous; grain, straight, close; rays, numerous, very obscure; non-resinous.

PHYSICAL QUALITIES: Light in weight (46th in this list); 28 lbs. per cu. ft.; sp. gr. 0.4621; strong (25th in this list); elastic (12th in this list); soft (50th in this list); shrinkage 3 or 4 per cent.; warps little; durable; easily worked; splits easily.

COMMON USES: Matches (almost exclusively on the Pacific Coast), interior finish, ship and boat building.

REMARKS: Resin, a powerful diuretic and insecticide.

27

RED CEDAR.

Juniperus virginiana Linnaeus.

Juniperus, the classical Latin name; virginiana, in honor of the State of Virginia.

HABITAT: (See map); best in Gulf States in swamps, especially on the west coast of Florida.

CHARACTERISTICS OF THE TREE: Height, 40'-50', even 80'; diameter, 1'-2'; trunk, ridged, sometimes expanded; branches, low; bark, light brown, loose, ragged, separating into long, narrow, persistent, stringy scales; leaves, opposite, of two kinds, awl-shaped, and scale-shaped; fruit, dark blue berry.

APPEARANCE OF WOOD: Color, dull red, sap-wood white; non-porous; rings, easily distinguished; grain, straight; rays, numerous, very obscure; non-resinous.

PHYSICAL QUALITIES: Very light in weight (42d in this list); 30 lbs. per cu. ft.; sp. gr. 0.4826; medium strong (43d in this list); brittle (61st in this list); medium hard (34th in this list); shrinkage, 3 per cent.; warps little; very durable; easy to work; splits readily, takes nails well.

COMMON USES: Pencils, chests, cigar boxes, pails, interior finish.

REMARKS: Fragrant. Pencils are made almost exclusively of this wood, because it is light, strong, stiff, straight and fine-grained and easily whittled; supply being rapidly depleted.

28

BLACK WILLOW.

Salix nigra Marshall.

Salix, from two Celtic words meaning near-water; nigra refers to the dark bark.

HABITAT: (See map); grows largest in southern Illinois, Indiana and Texas, on moist banks.

CHARACTERISTICS OF THE TREE: Height, 30'-40', sometimes 120'; diameter, 1'-2', rarely 3'-4'; stout, upright, spreading branches, from common base; bark, rough and dark brown or black, often tinged with yellow or brown; leaves, lanceolate, often scythe-shaped, serrate edges; fruit, a capsule containing small, hairy seeds.

APPEARANCE OF WOOD: Color, light reddish brown, sap-wood, thin, whitish; diffuse-porous; rings, obscure; grain, close and weak; rays, obscure.

PHYSICAL QUALITIES: Light in weight (51st in this list); 27.77 lbs. per cu. ft.; sp. gr. 0.4456; weak (65th in this list); very brittle (64th in this list); soft (46th in this list); shrinks considerably; warps and checks badly; soft, weak, indents without breaking; splits easily.

COMMON USES: Lap-boards, baskets, water wheels, fuel and charcoal for gunpowder.

REMARKS: Its characteristic of indenting without breaking has given it use as lining for carts and as cricket bats. Of the many willows, the most tree like in proportion in eastern North America. Bark contains salycylic acid.

BUTTERNUT. WHITE WALNUT.

Butternut, because the nuts are rich in oil.

Juglans cinerea Linnaeus.

Juglans means Jove's nut; cinerea refers to ash-colored bark.

HABITAT:: (See map); best in Ohio basin.

CHARACTERISTICS OF THE TREE: Height, 75'-100'; diameter, 2'-4'; branches low, broad spreading deep roots; bark, grayish brown, deep fissures broad ridges; leaves 15"-30" long, compound 11 to 17 leaflets, hairy and rough; fruit, oblong, pointed, edible, oily nut.

APPEARANCE OF WOOD: Color, light brown, darkening with exposure, sapwood whitish; diffuse, porous; rings, not prominent; grain, fairly straight, coarse, takes high polish; rays, distinct, thin, obscure.

PHYSICAL QUALITIES: Light in weight (56th in this list); 25 lbs. per cu. ft.; sp. gr. 0.4086; weak (57th in this list); elasticity, medium (52d in this list); soft (47th in this list); shrinkage .... per cent.; warps little; durable; easy to work; splits easily.

COMMON USES: Cabinet work, inside trim.

REMARKS: Green husks of fruit give yellow dye. Sugar made from sap.

BLACK WALNUT.

Juglans nigra Linnaeus.

Juglans means Jove's nut; nigra refers to the dark wood.

HABITAT: (See map); best in western North Carolina and Tennessee.

CHARACTERISTICS OF THE TREE: Height, 90'-120', even 150'; diameter, 3' to even 8'; clean of branches for 50' to 60'; bark, brownish, almost black, deep fissures, and broad, rounded ridges; leaves, 1'-2' long, compound pinnate, 15 to 23 leaflets, fall early; fruit, nut, with adherent husk, and edible kernel.

APPEARANCE OF WOOD: Color, chocolate brown, sap-wood much lighter; diffuse-porous; rings, marked by slightly larger pores; grain, straight; rays, numerous, thin, not conspicuous.

PHYSICAL QUALITIES: Weight, medium (31st in this list); 38 lbs. per cu. ft.; sp. gr. 0.6115; strong (32d in this list); elastic (23d in this list); hard (21st in this list); shrinkage, 5 per cent.; warps little; very durable; easy to work; splits with some difficulty, takes and holds nails well.

COMMON USES: Gun stocks (since 17th century), veneers, cabinet making.

REMARKS: Formerly much used for furniture, now scarce. Plentiful in California. Most valuable wood of North American forests. Wood superior to European variety.

31

MOCKERNUT. BLACK HICKORY. BULL-NUT. BIG-BUD HICKORY. WHITE-HEART HICKORY. KING NUT.

Mockernut refers to disappointing character of nuts.

Hicoria alba (Linnaeus) Britton. Carya tomentosa Nuttall.

Hicoria, shortened and latinized from Pawcohicora, the Indian name for the liquor obtained from the kernels; alba refers to the white wood, carya, the Greek name for walnut; tomentosa refers to hairy under surface of leaf.

HABITAT: (See map); best in lower Ohio valley, Missouri and Arkansas.

CHARACTERISTICS OF THE TREE: Height, 75', rarely 100'; diameter, 2'-3'; rises high in forest; bark, dark gray, shallow, irregular interrupted fissures, rough but not shaggy in old trees; leaves, 8"-12" long, compound, 7-9 leaflets, fragrant when crushed; fruit, spherical nut, thick shell, edible kernel.

APPEARANCE OF WOOD: Color, dark brown, sap-wood nearly white; ring-porous; rings, marked by few large regularly distributed open ducts; grain, usually straight, close; rays, numerous, thin, obscure.

PHYSICAL QUALITIES: Very heavy (3d in this list); 53 lbs. per cu. ft.; sp. gr., 0.8218; very strong (11th in this list); very elastic (14th in this list); very hard (3d in this list); shrinkage, 10 per cent.; warps ....; not durable; very hard to work; splits with great difficulty, almost impossible to nail.

COMMON USES: Wheels, runners, tool and axe handles, agricultural implements.

REMARKS: Confounded commercially with shellbark hickory.

32

SHELLBARK HICKORY. SHAGBARK HICKORY.

Hicoria ovata (Millar) Britton. Carya alba Nuttall.

Hickory is shortened and latinized from Pawcohicora, the Indian name for the liquor obtained from the kernels; ovata refers to oval nut; carya, the Greek name for walnut.

HABITAT: (See map); best in lower Ohio valley.

CHARACTERISTICS OF THE TREE: Height, 70'-90' and even 120'; diameter, 2'-3', even 4'; straight, columnar trunk; bark, dark gray, separates into long, hard, plate-like strips, which cling to tree by middle, on young trees very smooth and close; leaves, 8"-20" long, compound 5 or (7) leaflets; nuts, globular, husk, four-valved, split easily, thin-shelled, edible.

APPEARANCE OF WOOD: Color, reddish brown, sap-wood whitish; ring-porous; rings, clearly marked; grain, straight; rays, numerous, thin.

PHYSICAL QUALITIES: Very Heavy (1st in this list); 51 lbs. per cu. ft.; sp. gr., 0.8372; very strong (5th in this list); very elastic (7th in this list); very hard (5th in this list); shrinkage, 10 per cent.; warps badly; not very durable under exposure; hard to work, very tough; hard to split, very difficult to nail.

COMMON USES: Agricultural implements, handles, wheel spokes.

REMARKS: American hickory is famous both for buggies and ax handles, because it is flexible and very tough in resistance to blows.

33

PIGNUT.

Nuts eaten by swine.

Hicoria glabra (Miller) Britton. Carya porcina.

Hicoria is shortened and latinized from Pawcohicora, the Indian name for the liquor obtained from the kernel; glabra refers to smooth bark; Carya the Greek name for walnut; porcina means pertaining to hogs.

HABITAT: (See map); best in lower Ohio valley.

CHARACTERISTICS OF THE TREE: Height, 80'-100'; diameter 2'-4'; trunk often forked; bark, light gray, shallow fissures, rather smooth, rarely exfoliates; leaves, 8"-12" long, compound 7 leaflets, sharply serrate; fruit, a thick-shelled nut, bitter kernel.

APPEARANCE OF WOOD: Color, light or dark brown, the thick sap-wood lighter, often nearly white; ring-porous; rings marked by many large open ducts; grain, straight; rays, small and insignificant.

PHYSICAL QUALITIES: Very heavy (4th in this list); 56 lbs. per cu. ft.; sp. gr., 0.8217; very strong (15th in this list); elastic (27th in this list); very hard (2d in this list); shrinkage, 10 per cent.; warps ....; hard to work; splits with difficulty, hard to drive nails into.

COMMON USES: Agricultural implements, wheels, runners, tool handles.

REMARKS: Wood not distinguished from shellbark hickory in commerce.

34

BLUE BEECH. HORNBEAM. WATER BEECH. IRON-WOOD.

Blue refers to color of bark; the trunk resembles beech; horn refers to horny texture of wood.

Carpinus caroliniana Walter.

Carpinus, classical Latin name; caroliniana, named from the state.

HABITAT: (See map); best on western slopes of Southern Allegheny Mountains and in southern Arkansas and Texas.

CHARACTERISTICS OF THE TREE: Height, a small tree, 30'-50' high; diameter, 6"-2'; short, fluted, sinewy trunk; bark, smooth, bluish gray; leaves, falcate, doubly serrate; fruit, small oval nut, enclosed in leaf-like bract.

APPEARANCE OF WOOD: Color, light brown, sap-wood thick, whitish; diffuse-porous; rings, obscure; grain, close; rays, numerous, broad.

PHYSICAL QUALITIES: Heavy (13th in this list); 45 lbs. per cu. ft.; sp. gr. 0.7286; very strong (9th in this list); very stiff (15th in this list); hard (14th in this list); shrinkage, 6 per cent.; warps and checks badly; not durable; hard to work; splits with great difficulty.

COMMON USES: Levers, tool handles.

REMARKS: No other wood so good for levers, because of stiffness.

35

CANOE BIRCH. WHITE BIRCH. PAPER BIRCH.

All names refer to bark.

Betula papyrifera Marshall.

Betula, the classical Latin name; papyrifera refers to paper bearing bark.

HABITAT: (See map); best west of Rocky Mountains.

CHARACTERISTICS OF THE TREE: Height, 60'-80'; diameter, 2'-3'; stem rarely quite straight; bark, smooth, white, exterior marked with lenticels, peeling freely horizontally into thin papery layers, showing brown or orange beneath, contains oil which burns hotly, formerly used by Indians for canoes, very remarkable (see Keeler, page 304); leaves, heart-shaped, irregularly serrate; fruit, pendulous strobiles.

APPEARANCE OF WOOD: Color, brown or reddish, sap-wood white; diffuse-porous; rings, obscure; grain, fairly straight; rays, numerous, obscure.

PHYSICAL QUALITIES: Weight, medium (33d in this list); 37 lbs. per cu. ft.; sp. gr. 0.5955; very strong (14th in this list); very elastic (2d in this list); medium hard (39th in this list); shrinkage, 6 per cent.; warps, ...; not durable, except bark; easy to work; splits with difficulty, nails well, tough.

COMMON USES: Spools, shoe lasts and pegs, turnery, bark for canoes.

REMARKS: Forms forests. Sap yields syrup. Bark yields starch. Valuable to woodsmen in many ways.

36

RED BIRCH. RIVER BIRCH.

Red refers to color of bark; river, prefers river bottoms.

Betula nigra Linnaeus.

Betula, the classical Latin name.

HABITAT: (See map); best in Florida, Louisiana and Texas.

CHARACTERISTICS OF THE TREE: Height, 30'-80', and even higher; diameter, 1', even 5'; trunk, often divided low; bark, dark brown, marked by horizontal lenticels, peels into paper plates, curling back; leaves, doubly serrate, often almost lobed; fruit, pubescent, erect, strobiles.

APPEARANCE OF WOOD: Color, light brown, thick sap-wood, whitish; diffuse-porous; rings, not plain; grain, close, rather crooked; rays, numerous, obscure.

PHYSICAL QUALITIES: Weight, medium (36th in this list); 35 lbs. per cu. ft.; sp. gr. 0.5762; strong (22d in this list); very elastic (19th in this list); medium hard (37th in this list); shrinkage, 6 per cent.; warps, ...; not durable when exposed; hard to work, tough; splits with difficulty, nails well.

COMMON USES: Shoe lasts, yokes, furniture.

REMARKS: Prefers moist land.

37

CHERRY BIRCH. SWEET BIRCH. BLACK BIRCH. MAHOGANY BIRCH.

Cherry, because bark resembles that of cherry tree; sweet, refers to the taste of the spicy bark.

Betula lenta Linnaeus.

Betula, the classical Latin name; lenta, meaning tenacious, sticky, may refer to the gum which exudes from the trunk.

HABITAT: (See map); best in Tennessee Mountains.

CHARACTERISTICS OF THE TREE: Height, 50'-80'; diameter, 2'-5'; trunk, rarely straight; bark, dark reddish brown, on old trunks deeply furrowed and broken into thick, irregular plates, marked with horizontal lenticels; resembles cherry; spicy, aromatic; leaves, ovate, oblong, 2"-6" long, irregularly serrate; fruit, erect strobiles.

APPEARANCE OF WOOD: Color, dark, reddish brown; diffuse-porous; rings, obscure; grain, close, satiny, polishes well, often stained to imitate mahogany; rays, numerous, obscure.

PHYSICAL QUALITIES: Heavy (6th in this list); 47 lbs. per cu. ft.; sp. gr., 0.7617; very strong (4th in this list); very elastic (6th in this list); hard (11th in this list); shrinkage, 6 per cent.; warps, little; not durable if exposed; rather hard to work; splits hard, tough.

COMMON USES: Dowel pins, wooden ware, boats and ships.

REMARKS: The birches are not usually distinguished from one another in the market.

38

YELLOW BIRCH. GRAY BIRCH.

Yellow and gray, both refer to the color of the bark.

Betula lutea F. A. Michaux.

Betula, the classical Latin name; lutea refers to the yellow color of the bark.

HABITAT: (See map); best in northern New York and New England.

CHARACTERISTICS OF THE TREE: Height, 60'-100'; diameter, 3'-4'; branches, low; bark, silvery, yellow, gray, peeling horizontally into thin, papery, persistent layers, but on very old trunks, there are rough, irregular, plate-like scales; leaves, ovate, sharply, doubly serrate; fruit, erect, 1" strobiles.

APPEARANCE OF WOOD: Color, light reddish brown, sap-wood white; diffuse-porous; rings, obscure; grain, close, fairly straight; rays, numerous, obscure.

PHYSICAL QUALITIES: Heavy (21st in this list); 40 lbs. per cu. ft.; sp. gr., 0.6553; very strong (2nd in this list); very elastic (2d in this list); medium hard (22d in this list); shrinkage, 6 per cent.; warps ....; not durable; rather hard to work, polishes well; splits with difficulty, holds nails well.

COMMON USES: Furniture, spools, button molds, shoe lasts, shoe pegs, pill boxes, yokes.

REMARKS: The birches are not usually distinguished from one another in the market.

39

BEECH.

Fagus grandifolia Ehrhart. Fagus americana Sweet. Fagus ferruginea Aiton. Fagus atropunicea (Marshall) Sudworth.

Fagus (Greek phago means to eat), refers to edible nut; ferruginea, refers to the iron rust color of the leaves in the fall; atropunicea, meaning dark red or purple, may refer to the color of the leaves of the copper beech.

HABITAT: (See map); best in southern Alleghany Mountains and lower Ohio valley.

CHARACTERISTICS OF THE TREE: Height, 70'-80' and even 120'; diameter, 3'-4'; in forest, trunk tall, slender, sinewy; bark, smooth, ashy gray; leaves, feather-veined, wedge-shaped, serrate; leaf buds, long, pointed; fruit, 2 small triangular nuts, enclosed in burr, seeds about once in 3 years.

APPEARANCE OF WOOD: Color, reddish, variable, sap-wood white; diffuse-porous; rings, obscure; grain, straight; rays, broad, very conspicuous.

PHYSICAL QUALITIES: Heavy (20th in this list); 42 lbs. per cu. ft.; sp. gr., 0.6883; very strong (10th in this list); elastic (13th in this list); hard (22d in this list); shrinkage, 5 per cent.; warps and checks during seasoning; not durable; hard to work, takes fine polish; splits with difficulty, hard to nail.

COMMON USES: Plane stocks, shoe lasts, tool handles, chairs.

REMARKS: Often forms pure forests. Uses due to its hardness.

40

CHESTNUT.

Castanea dentata (Marshall) Borkhausen.

Castanea, the classical Greek and Latin name; dentata, refers to toothed leaf.

HABITAT: (See map); best in western North Carolina, and eastern Tennessee.

CHARACTERISTICS OF THE TREE: Height, 75'-100'; diameter, 3'-4', and even 12'; branches, low; bark, thick, shallow, irregular, fissures, broad, grayish brown ridges; leaves, lanceolate, coarsely serrate, midribs and veins prominent; fruit, nuts, thin-shelled, sweet, enclosed in prickly burrs.

APPEARANCE OF WOOD: Color, reddish brown, sap-wood lighter; ring-porous; rings, plain, pores large; grain, straight; rays, numerous, obscure.

PHYSICAL QUALITIES: Weight, light (50th in this list); 28 lbs. per cu. ft.; sp. gr., 0.4504; medium strong (46th in this list); elasticity, medium (46th in this list); medium hard (44th in this list); shrinkage, 6 per cent.; warps badly; very durable, especially in contact with soil, fairly easy to plane, chisel and saw; splits easily.

COMMON USES: Railway ties, fence posts, interior finish.

REMARKS: Grows rapidly, and lives to great age. Wood contains much tannic acid. Uses depend largely upon its durability. Lately whole regions depleted by fungous pest.

41

RED OAK.

Quercus rubra Linnaeus.

Quercus, the classical Latin name; rubra, refers to red color of wood.

HABITAT: (See map); best in Massachusetts and north of the Ohio river.

CHARACTERISTICS OF THE TREE: Height, 70'-100', even 150'; diameter, 3'-6'; a tall, handsome tree, branches rather low; bark, brownish gray, broad, thin, rounded ridges, rather smooth; leaves, 7 to 9 triangular pointed lobes, with rounded sinuses; acorns, characteristically large, in flat shallow cups.

APPEARANCE OF WOOD: Color, reddish brown, sap-wood darker; ring-porous; rings, marked by several rows of very large open ducts; grain, crooked, coarse; rays, few, but broad, conspicuous.

PHYSICAL QUALITIES: Heavy (23d in this list); 45 lbs. per cu. ft.; sp. gr., 0.6540; strong (21st in this list); elastic (18th in this list); hard (26th in this list); shrinkage 6 to 10 per cent.; warps and checks badly; moderately durable; easier to work than white oak; splits readily, nails badly.

COMMON USES: Cooperage, interior finish, furniture.

REMARKS: Grows rapidly. An inferior substitute for white oak. Bark used in tanning.

42

BLACK OAK. YELLOW BARK OAK.

Black refers to color of outer bark; yellow bark, refers to the inner bark, which is orange yellow.

Quercus velutina Lamarck. Quercus tinctoria Michaux.

Quercus, the classical Latin name; velutina, refers to the velvety surface of the young leaf; tinctoria, refers to dye obtained from inner bark.

HABITAT: (See map); best in lower Ohio valley.

CHARACTERISTICS OF THE TREE: Height, 70'-80', even 150'; diameter 3'-4'; branches, low; bark, dark gray to black, deep fissures, broad, rounded, firm ridges, inner bark, yellow, yielding dye; leaves, large, lustrous, leathery, of varied forms; acorns, small; kernel, yellow, bitter.

APPEARANCE OF WOOD: Color, reddish brown, sap-wood lighter; ring-porous; rings, marked by several rows of very large open ducts; grain, crooked; rays, thin.

PHYSICAL QUALITIES: Heavy (17th in this list); 45 lbs. per cu. ft.; sp. gr., 0.7045; very strong (17th in this list); elastic (25th in this list); hard (18th in this list); shrinkage, 4 per cent. or more; warps and checks in drying; durable; rather hard to work; splits readily, nails badly.

COMMON USES: Furniture, interior trim, cooperage, construction.

REMARKS: Foliage handsome in fall; persists thru winter.

43

BASKET OAK. COW OAK.

Cow refers to the fact that its acorns are eaten by cattle.

Quercus michauxii Nuttall.

Quercus, the classical Latin name; michauxii, named for the botanist Michaux.

HABITAT: (See map); best in Arkansas and Louisiana, especially in river bottoms.

CHARACTERISTICS OF THE TREE: Height, 80'-100'; diameter 3', even 7'; trunk, often clean and straight for 40' or 50'; bark, conspicuous, light gray, rough with loose ashy gray, scaly ridges; leaves, obovate, regularly scalloped; acorns, edible for cattle.

APPEARANCE OF WOOD: Color, light brown, sap-wood light buff; ring-porous; rings, marked by few rather large, open ducts; grain, likely to be crooked; rays, broad, conspicuous.

PHYSICAL QUALITIES: Very heavy (5th in this list); 46 lbs. per cu. ft.; sp. gr., 0.8039; very strong (12th in this list); elastic (33d in this list); hard (10th in this list); shrinkage, 4 per cent. or more; warps unless carefully seasoned; durable; hard and tough to work; splits easily, bad to nail.

COMMON USES: Construction, agricultural implements, wheel stock, baskets.

REMARKS: The best white oak of the south. Not distinguished from white oak in the market.

44

BUR OAK. MOSSY-CUP OAK. OVER-CUP OAK.

Quercus macrocarpa Michaux.

Quercus, the classical Latin name; macrocarpa, refers to the large acorn.

HABITAT: (See map); best in southern Indiana, Illinois and Kansas.

CHARACTERISTICS OF THE TREE: Height, 70'-130', even 170'; diameter, 5'-7'; branches, high; corky wings on young branches; bark, gray brown, deeply furrowed; deep opposite sinuses on large leaves; acorns, half enclosed in mossy-fringed cup.

APPEARANCE OF WOOD: Color, rich brown, sap-wood, thin, lighter; ring-porous; rings, marked by 1 to 3 rows of small open ducts; grain, crooked; rays, broad, and conspicuous.

PHYSICAL QUALITIES: Heavy (9th in this list); 46 lbs. per cu. ft.; sp. gr., 0.7453; very strong (16th in this list); elastic (37th in this list); hard (9th in this list); shrinkage, 4 per cent. or more; warps, ...; hard, and tough to work; splits easily, resists nailing.

COMMON USES: Ship building, cabinet work, railway ties, cooperage.

REMARKS: Good for prairie planting. One of the most valuable woods of North America. Not distinguished from White Oak in commerce.

45

WHITE OAK (Western).

Quercus garryana Douglas.

Quercus, the classical Latin name; garryana, named for Garry.

HABITAT: (See map); best in western Washington and Oregon.

CHARACTERISTICS OF THE TREE: Height, 60'-70', even 100'; diameter, 2'-3'; branches, spreading; bark, light brown, shallow fissures, broad ridges; leaves, coarsely pinnatified, lobed; fruit, large acorns.

APPEARANCE OF WOOD: Color, light brown, sap-wood whitish; ring-porous; rings, marked by 1 to 3 rows of open ducts; grain, close, crooked; rays, varying greatly in width, often conspicuous.

PHYSICAL QUALITIES: Heavy (10th in this list); 46 lbs. per cu. ft.; sp. gr., 0.7449; strong (28th in this list); elasticity medium (54th in this list); hard (8th in this list); shrinkage, 5 or 6 per cent.; warps, unless carefully seasoned; durable; hard to work, very tough; splits badly in nailing.

COMMON USES: Ship building, vehicles, furniture, interior finish.

REMARKS: Best of Pacific oaks. Shrubby at high elevations.

POST OAK.

Quercus stellata Wangenheim. Quercus minor (Marsh) Sargent. Quercus obtusiloba Michaux.

Quercus, the classical Latin name; stellata, refers to the stellate hairs on upper side of leaf; minor, refers to size of tree, which is often shrubby; obtusiloba, refers to the blunt lobes of leaves.

HABITAT: (See map); best in Mississippi basin.

CHARACTERISTICS OF THE TREE: Height, 50'-75', even 100'; but often a shrub; diameter, 2'-3'; branches, spreading into dense round-topped head; bark, red or brown, deep, vertical, almost continuous, fissures and broad ridges, looks corrugated; leaves, in large tufts at ends of branchlets; acorns, small, sessile.

APPEARANCE OF WOOD: Color, brown, thick, sap-wood, lighter; ring-porous; rings, 1 to 3 rows of not large open ducts; grain, crooked; rays, numerous, conspicuous.

PHYSICAL QUALITIES: Very heavy (2d in this list); 50 lbs. per cu. ft.; sp. gr., 0.8367; strong (29th in this list); medium elastic (50th in this list); very hard (4th in this list); shrinkage, 4 per cent. or more; warps and checks badly in seasoning; durable; hard to work; splits readily, bad to nail.

COMMON USES: Cooperage, railway ties, fencing, construction.

REMARKS: Wood often undistinguished from white oak.

WHITE OAK. STAVE OAK.

Quercus alba Linnaeus.

Quercus, the classical Latin name; white and alba, refer to white bark.

HABITAT: (See map); best on western slopes of Southern Alleghany Mountains, and in lower Ohio river valley.

CHARACTERISTICS OF THE TREE: Height, 80'-100'; diameter, 3'-5'; trunk, in forest, tall, in open, short; bark, easily distinguished, light gray with shallow fissures, scaly; leaves, rounded lobes, and sinuses; acorns, 3/4" to 1" long, ripen first year.

APPEARANCE OF WOOD: Color, light brown, sap-wood paler; ring-porous; rings, plainly defined by pores; grain crooked; rays, broad, very conspicuous and irregular.

PHYSICAL QUALITIES: Heavy (8th in this list); 50 lbs. per cu. ft.; sp. gr., 0.7470; strong (23d in this list); elastic (32d in this list); hard (13th in this list); shrinkage, from 4 to 10 per cent.; warps and checks considerably, unless carefully seasoned; very durable, hard to work; splits somewhat hard, very difficult to nail.

COMMON USES: Interior finish, furniture, construction, ship building, farm implements, cabinet making.

REMARKS: The most important of American oaks.

48

CORK ELM. ROCK ELM. HICKORY ELM. WHITE ELM. CLIFF ELM.

Cork refers to corky ridges on branches.

Ulmus thomasi Sargent. Ulmus racemosa Thomas.

Ulmus, the classical Latin name; racemosa, refers to racemes of flowers.

HABITAT: (See map); best in Ontario and southern Michigan.

CHARACTERISTICS OF THE TREE: Height, 80'-100'; diameter, 2'-3', trunk often clear for 60'; bark, gray tinged with red, corky, irregular projections, give shaggy appearance; leaves, obovate, doubly serrate, 3"-4" long; fruit, pubescent, samaras.

APPEARANCE OF WOOD: Color, light brown or red; sap-wood yellowish; ring-porous; rings, marked with one or two rows of small open ducts; grain, interlaced; rays, numerous, obscure.

PHYSICAL QUALITIES: Heavy (15th in this list); 45 lbs. per cu. ft.; sp. gr., 0.7263; very strong (13th in this list); elastic (22d in this list); hard (15th in this list); shrinkage, 5 per cent.; warps, ...; very durable; hard to work; splits and nails with difficulty.

COMMON USES: Hubs, agricultural implements, sills, bridge timbers.

REMARKS: The best of the elm woods.

49

WHITE ELM. AMERICAN ELM. WATER ELM.

Water, because it flourishes on river banks.

Ulmus americana Linnaeus.

Ulmus, the classical Latin name.

HABITAT: (See map); best northward on river bottoms.

CHARACTERISTICS OF THE TREE: Height, 90', even 120'; diameter, 3'-8'; trunk, usually divides at 30'-40' from ground into upright branches, making triangular outline; bark, ashy gray, deep longitudinal fissures, broad ridges; leaves, 4"-6" long, oblique obovate, doubly serrate, smooth one way; fruit, small, roundish, flat, smooth, samaras.

APPEARANCE OF WOOD: Color, light brown, sap-wood yellowish; ring-porous; rings, marked by several rows of large open ducts; grain, interlaced; rays, numerous, thin.

PHYSICAL QUALITIES: Heavy (24th in this list); 34 lbs. per cu. ft.; sp. gr., 0.6506; strong (33d in this list); elasticity, medium (59th in this list); medium hard (28th in this list); shrinkage, 5 per cent.; warps ....; not durable; hard to work, tough, will not polish; splits with difficulty.

COMMON USES: Cooperage, wheel stock, flooring.

REMARKS: Favorite ornamental tree, but shade light, and leaves fall early.

50

CUCUMBER TREE. MOUNTAIN MAGNOLIA.

Cucumber, refers to the shape of the fruit.

Magnolia acuminata Linnaeus.

Magnolia, named for Pierre Magnol, a French botanist; acuminata, refers to pointed fruit.

HABITAT: (See map); best at the base of mountains in North Carolina and South Carolina and Tennessee.

CHARACTERISTICS OF THE TREE: Height, 60'-90'; diameter, 3'-4'; in forest, clear trunk for 2/3 of height (40' or 50'); bark, dark brown, thick, furrowed; leaves, large, smooth; flowers, large greenish yellow; fruit, dark red "cones" formed of two seeded follicles.

APPEARANCE OF WOOD: Color, yellow brown, thick sapwood, lighter; diffuse-porous; rings, obscure; grain, very straight, close, satiny; rays, numerous thin.

PHYSICAL QUALITIES: Light (45th in this list); .... lbs. per cu. ft.; sp. gr., 0.4690; medium strong (49th in this list); elastic (38th in this list); medium hard (41st in this list); shrinkage, 5 per cent.; warps ....; very durable; easy to work; splits easily, takes nails well.

COMMON USES: Pump logs, cheap furniture, shelving.

REMARKS: Wood similar to yellow poplar, and often sold with it.

51

YELLOW POPLAR. WHITEWOOD. TULIP TREE.

Poplar, inappropriate, inasmuch as the tree does not belong to poplar family. White, refers inappropriately to the color of the wood, which is greenish yellow.

Liriodendron tulipifera Linnaeus.

Liriodendron, means lily-tree; tulipifera means tulip-bearing.

HABITAT: (See map); best in lower Ohio valley and southern Appalachian mountains.

CHARACTERISTICS OF THE TREE: Height, 70'-90'; even 200'; diameter, 6'-8', even 12'; tall, magnificent trunk, unsurpassed in grandeur by any eastern American tree; bark, brown, aromatic, evenly furrowed so as to make clean, neat-looking trunk; leaves, 4 lobed, apex, peculiarly truncated, clean cut; flowers, tulip-like; fruit, cone, consisting of many scales.

APPEARANCE OF WOOD: Color, light greenish or yellow brown, sap-wood, creamy white; diffuse-porous; rings, close but distinct; grain, straight; rays, numerous and plain.

PHYSICAL QUALITIES: Light (54th in this list); 26 lbs. per cu. ft.; sp. gr., 0.4230; medium strong (51st in this list); elastic (39th in this list); soft (49th in this list); shrinkage, 5 per cent.; warps little; durable; easy to work; brittle and does not split readily, nails very well.

COMMON USES: Construction work, furniture, interiors, boats, carriage bodies, wooden pumps.

REMARKS: Being substituted largely for white pine.

52

SWEET GUM. Gum, refers to exudations.

Liquidambar styraciflua Linnaeus.

Liquidambar, means liquid gum; styraciflua, means fluid resin (storax).

HABITAT: (See map); best in the lower Mississippi valley.

CHARACTERISTICS OF THE TREE: Height, 80'-140'; diameter, 3'-5'; trunk, tall, straight; bark, light brown tinged with red, deeply fissured; branchlets often having corky wings; leaves, star-shaped, five pointed; conspicuously purple and crimson in autumn; fruit, multi-capsular, spherical, persistent heads.

APPEARANCE OF WOOD: Color, light red brown, sap-wood almost white; diffuse-porous; rings, fine and difficult to distinguish; grain, straight, close, polishes well; rays, numerous, very obscure.

PHYSICAL QUALITIES: Weight, medium (34th in this list); 37 lbs. per cu. ft.; sp. gr., 0.5909; medium strong (52d in this list); elasticity medium (44th in this list); medium hard (36th in this list); shrinkage, 6 per cent.; warps and twists badly in seasoning; not durable when exposed; easy to work; crumbles in splitting; nails badly.

COMMON USES: Building construction, cabinet-work, veneering, street pavement, barrel staves and heads.

REMARKS: Largely used in veneers, because when solid it warps and twists badly. Exudations used in medicine to some extent.

53

SYCAMORE. BUTTONWOOD. BUTTON BALL. WATER BEECH.

Sycamore, from two Greek words meaning fig and mulberry; buttonwood and button-ball, refer to fruit balls.

Platanus occidentalis Linnaeus.

Platanus, refers to the broad leaves; occidentalis, western, to distinguish it from European species.

HABITAT: (See map); best in valley of lower Ohio and Mississippi.

CHARACTERISTICS OF THE TREE: Height, 70'-100', and even 170'; diameter, 6'-12'; trunk, commonly divides into 2 or 3 large branches, limbs spreading, often dividing angularly; bark, flakes off in great irregular masses, leaving mottled surface, greenish gray and brown, this peculiarity due to its rigid texture; leaves, palmately 3 to 5 lobed, 4"-9" long, petiole enlarged, enclosing buds; fruit, large rough balls, persistent through winter.

APPEARANCE OF WOOD: Color, reddish brown, sap-wood lighter; diffuse-porous; rings, marked by broad bands of small ducts; grain, cross, close; rays, numerous, large, conspicuous.

PHYSICAL QUALITIES: Weight, medium (38th in this list); 35 lbs. per cu. ft.; sp. gr., 0.5678; medium strong (54th in this list); elasticity, medium (43d in this list); medium hard (30th in this list); shrinkage, 5 per cent.; warps little; very durable, once used for mummy coffins; hard to work; splits very hard.

COMMON USES: Tobacco boxes, yokes, furniture, butcher blocks.

REMARKS: Trunks often very large and hollow.

54

WILD BLACK CHERRY.

Padus serotina (Ehrhart) Agardh. Prunus serotina Ehrhart.

Padus, the old Greek name; prunus, the classical Latin name; serotina, because it blossoms late (June).

HABITAT: (See map); best on southern Allegheny mountains.

CHARACTERISTICS OF THE TREE: Height, 40'-50', even 100'; diameter, 2'-4'; straight, columnar trunk, often free from branches for 70'; bark, blackish and rough, fissured in all directions, broken into small, irregular, scaly plates, with raised edges; leaves, oblong to lanceolate, deep, shiny green; fruit, black drupe, 1/2".

APPEARANCE OF WOOD: Color, light brown or red, sap-wood yellow; diffuse-porous; rings, obscure; grain, straight, close, fine, takes fine polish; rays, numerous.

PHYSICAL QUALITIES: Weight, medium (35th in this list); 36 lbs. per cu. ft.; sp. gr., 0.5822; strong (35th in this list); elasticity medium (45th in this list); hard (16th in this list); shrinkage, 5 per cent.; warps, little; durability ....; easily worked; splits easily, must be nailed with care.

COMMON USES: Cabinet-work, costly interior trim.

REMARKS: Grows rapidly.

55

BLACK LOCUST. LOCUST. YELLOW LOCUST.

Yellow, from color of sap-wood.

Robinia pseudacacia Linnaeus.

Robinia, in honor of Jean Robin, of France; pseudacacia, means false acacia.

HABITAT: (See map); best on western Allegheny mountains in West Virginia.

CHARACTERISTICS OF THE TREE: Height, 50'-80'; diameter, 3'-4'; bark, strikingly deeply furrowed, dark brown; prickles on small branches, grows fast, forms thickets, on account of underground shoots; leaves, 8"-14" long, pinnately compound; 7 to 9 leaflets, close at night and in rainy weather; fruit, pod 3"-4" long.

APPEARANCE OF WOOD: Color, brown, sap-wood thin, yellowish; ring-porous; rings, clearly marked by 2 or 3 rows of large open ducts; grain, crooked, compact.

PHYSICAL QUALITIES: Heavy (12th in this list); 45 lbs. per cu. ft.; sp. gr., 0.7333; very strong (1st in this list); elastic (9th in this list); very hard (6th in this list); shrinkage, 5 per cent.; warps badly, very durable; hard to work, tough; splits in nailing.

COMMON USES: Shipbuilding, construction, "tree-nails" or pins, wagon hubs.

REMARKS: Widely planted and cultivated east and west. Likely to be infested with borers.

56

MAHOGANY.

Swietenia mahagoni Jacquin.

Swietenia, in honor of Dr. Gerard Van Swieten of Austria; mahagoni, a South American word.

[Illustration: Habitat.]

HABITAT: (See map); only on Florida Keys in the United States.

CHARACTERISTICS OF THE TREE: Height, 40'-50'; diameter, 2' or more, foreign trees larger; immense buttresses at base of trunk; bark, thick, dark red-brown, having surface of broad, thick scales; leaves, 4"-6" long, compound, 4 pairs of leaflets; fruit, 4"-5" long, containing seeds.

APPEARANCE OF WOOD: Color, red-brown, sap-wood, thin, yellow; diffuse-porous; rings, inconspicuous; grain, crooked; rays, fine and scattered, but plain.

PHYSICAL QUALITIES: Heavy (14th in this list); 45 lbs. per cu. ft.; sp. gr., 0.7282; very strong (20th in this list); elastic (24th in this list); very hard (1st in this list); shrinkage, 5 per cent.; warps very little; very durable; genuine mahogany, hard to work; especially if grain is cross; somewhat brittle, and comparatively easy to split, nails with difficulty; polishes and takes glue well.

COMMON USES: Chiefly for cabinet-making, furniture, interior finishes and veneers.

REMARKS: Mahogany, now in great demand in the American market for fine furniture and interior trim comes from the West Indies, Central America and West Africa. The so-called Spanish mahogany, the most highly prized variety, came originally from the south of Hayti. The Honduras Mahogany was often called baywood. Botanically the varieties are not carefully distinguished; in the lumber yard the lumber is known by its sources. The Cuba wood can be partly distinguished by the white chalk-like specks in the pores and is cold to the touch, while the Honduras wood can be recognized by the black specks or lines in the grain. Both the Honduras and West India woods have a softer feel than the African wood, when rubbed with the thumb. The Cuba and St. Domingo wood are preferred to the Honduras, and still more to the African, but even experts have difficulty in distinguishing the varieties.

Spanish cedar, or furniture cedar (Cedrela odorata) belongs to the same family as mahogany and is often sold for it. It is softer, lighter, and easier to work.

57

OREGON MAPLE. WHITE MAPLE. LARGE LEAVED MAPLE.

Acer macrophyllum Pursh.

Acer, the classical Latin name; macrophyllum, refers to the large leaves.

HABITAT: (See map); best in southern Oregon.

CHARACTERISTICS OF THE TREE: Height, 70'-100'; diameter, 3'-5'; stout, often pendulous branches, making a handsome tree; bark, reddish brown, deeply furrowed, square scales; leaves, very large, 8"-12" and long petioles, deep, narrow sinuses; fruit, hairy samaras.

APPEARANCE OF WOOD: Color, rich brown and red, sap-wood thick, nearly white; diffuse-porous; rings, obscure; grain, close, fibres interlaced, sometimes figured, polishes well; rays, numerous and thin.

PHYSICAL QUALITIES: Light in weight (26th in this list); 30 lbs. per cu. ft.; sp. gr. 0.4909; medium strong (47th in this list); elasticity medium (57th in this list); medium hard (31st in this list); shrinkage, 4 per cent.; warps ....; not durable; rather hard to work; splits with difficulty.

COMMON USES: Tool and ax handles, furniture, interior finish.

REMARKS: A valuable wood on the Pacific coast.

58

SOFT MAPLE. WHITE MAPLE. SILVER MAPLE.

Silver, refers to white color of underside of leaf.

Acer saccharinum Linnaeus. Acer dasycarpum Ehrhart.

Acer, the classical Latin name; saccharinum, refers to sweetish juice; dasycarpum, refers to the wooliness of the fruit when young.

HABITAT: (See map); best in lower Ohio valley.

CHARACTERISTICS OF THE TREE: Height, 50'-90', even 120'; diameter, 3'-5'; form suggests elm; bark, reddish brown, furrowed, surface separating into large, loose scales; leaves, palmately 5 lobed, with narrow, acute sinuses, silvery white beneath, turn only yellow in autumn; fruit, divergent, winged samaras.

APPEARANCE OF WOOD: Color, brown and reddish, sap-wood, cream; diffuse-porous; rings, obscure; grain, twisted, wavy, fine, polishes well; rays, thin, numerous.

PHYSICAL QUALITIES: Weight, medium (40th in this list); 32 lbs. per cu. ft.; sp. gr., 0.5269; very strong (19th in this list); very elastic (20th in this list); hard (25th in this list); shrinkage, 5 per cent.; warps, ...; not durable under exposure; easily worked; splits in nailing.

COMMON USES: Flooring, furniture, turnery, wooden ware.

REMARKS: Grows rapidly. Curly varieties found. Sap produces some sugar.

59

RED MAPLE.

Acer rubrum Linnaeus.

Acer, the classical Latin name; rubrum, refers to red flowers and autumn leaves.

HABITAT: (See map); best in lower Ohio valley.

CHARACTERISTICS OF THE TREE: Height, 80'-120'; diameter, 2'-4'; branches, low; bark, dark gray, shaggy, divided by long ridges; leaves, palmately 5 lobed, acute sinuses; fruit, double samaras, forming characteristic maple key.

APPEARANCE OF WOOD: Color, light reddish brown, sap-wood, lighter; diffuse-porous; rings, obscure; grain, crooked; rays, numerous, obscure.

PHYSICAL QUALITIES: Weight, medium (30th in this list); 38 lbs. per cu. ft.; sp. gr., 0.6178; strong (36th in this list); elastic (36th in this list); hard (27th in this list); shrinkage, 5 per cent.; warps ....; not durable; fairly hard to work; splits with difficulty, splits badly in nailing.

COMMON USES: Flooring, turning, wooden ware.

REMARKS: Grows rapidly. Has red flowers, red keys, red leaf stems, and leaves scarlet or crimson in autumn.

HARD MAPLE. SUGAR MAPLE. ROCK MAPLE.

Acer saccharum Marshall.

Acer, the classical Latin name; saccharum, refers to sweet sap.

HABITAT: (See map); best in regions of Great Lakes.

CHARACTERISTICS OF THE TREE: Height, 100'-120'; diameter, 1-1/2'-3', even 4'; often trees in forest are without branches for 60'-70' from ground, in the open, large impressive tree; bark, gray brown, thick, deep, longitudinal fissures, hard and rough; leaves, opposite, 3 to 5 lobed, scarlet and yellow in autumn; fruit, double, slightly divergent samaras.

APPEARANCE OF WOOD: Color, light brown tinged with red; diffuse-porous rings, close but distinct; grain, crooked, fine, close, polishes well; rays, fine but conspicuous.

PHYSICAL QUALITIES: Heavy (19th in this list); 43 lbs. per cu. ft.; sp. gr., 0.6912; very strong (8th in this list); very elastic (5th in this list); very hard (7th in this list); shrinkage, 5 per cent.; warps badly; not durable when exposed; hard to work; splits badly in nailing.

COMMON USES: School and other furniture, car construction, carving, wooden type, tool handles, shoe lasts, piano actions, ships' keels.

REMARKS: Tree very tolerant. The uses of this wood are chiefly due to its hardness. Bird's-Eye Maple and Curly Maple are accidental varieties. Pure maple sugar is made chiefly from this species. Its ashes yield large quantities of potash.

BASSWOOD. LINDEN.

Bass, refers to bast or inner bark.

Tilia americana Linnaeus.

Tilia, the classical Latin name.

HABITAT: (See map); best in bottom lands of lower Ohio River.

CHARACTERISTICS OF THE TREE: Height, 60'-70', even 130'; diameter, 2'-4'; trunk, erect, pillar-like, branches spreading, making round heads; bark, light brown, furrowed, scaly surface, inner bark fibrous and tough, used for matting; leaves, oblique, heart-shaped, side nearest branch larger; fruit clustered on long pendulous stem, attached to vein of narrow bract.

APPEARANCE OF WOOD: Color, very light brown, approaching cream color, sap-wood, hardly distinguishable; diffuse-porous; rings, fine and close but clear; grain, straight; rays, numerous, obscure.

PHYSICAL QUALITIES: Light in weight (49th in this list); 28 lbs. per cu. ft.; sp. gr., 0.4525; weak (60th in this list); elasticity, medium (49th in this list); soft (64th in this list); shrinkage, 6 per cent.; warps comparatively little; quite durable; very easily worked; somewhat tough to split, nails well.

COMMON USES: Woodenware, carriage bodies, etc., picture molding, paper pulp, etc.

REMARKS: May be propagated by grafting as well as by seed. Is subject to attack by many insects. Wood used for carriage bodies because flexible and easily nailed.

62

SOUR GUM. TUPELO. PEPPERIDGE. BLACK GUM.

Tupelo, the Indian name.

Nyssa sylvatica Marshal.

Nyssa, from Nysa, the realm of moist vegetation and the home of Dio-nysus

(Bacchus) (the tree grows in low wet lands); sylvatica, refers to its habit of forest growth.

HABITAT: (See map); best in Southern Appalachian mountains.

CHARACTERISTICS OF THE TREE: Height, 40'-50', even 100'; diameter, 1'6"-3'6", even 5'; variable in form; bark, brown, deeply fissured and scaly; leaves, in sprays, short, petioled, brilliant scarlet in autumn; fruit, bluish black, sour, fleshy drupe.

APPEARANCE OF WOOD: Color, pale yellow, sap-wood, white, hardly distinguishable; diffuse-porous; rings, not plain; grain fine, twisted and interwoven; rays, numerous, thin.

PHYSICAL QUALITIES: Medium heavy (25th in this list); 39 lbs. per cu. ft.; sp. gr., 0.6356; strong (34th in this list); elasticity, medium (51st in this list); hard (20th in this list); shrinkage, 5 or 6 per cent.; warps and checks badly; not durable if exposed; hard to work; splits hard, tough.

COMMON USES: Wagon hubs, handles, yokes, wooden shoe soles, docks and wharves, rollers in glass factories.

REMARKS: The best grades closely resemble yellow poplar.

63

BLACK ASH. HOOP ASH.

Hoop, refers to its use for barrel hoops.

Fraxinus nigra Marshall. Fraxinus sambucifolia.

Fraxinus, from a Greek word (phraxis) meaning split, refers to the cleavability of the wood; sambucifolia, refers to the fact that the leaves are in odor like those of Elder (Sambucus).

HABITAT: (See map); best in moist places.

CHARACTERISTICS OF THE TREE: Height, 80'-90'; diameter, 1'-1-1/2'; slenderest of the forest trees, upright branches; bark, gray tinged with red, irregular plates, with thin scales; leaves, 10"-16" long, compound, 7 to 11 leaflets, in autumn rusty brown; fruit, single samaras in panicles.

APPEARANCE OF WOOD: Color, dark brown, sap-wood light; ring-porous; rings, well defined; grain, straight, burls often form highly prized veneers; rays, numerous and thin.

PHYSICAL QUALITIES: Medium heavy (27th in this list); 39 lbs. per cu. ft.; sp. gr., 0.6318; strong (38th in this list); elasticity, medium (12th in this list); hard (23d in this list); shrinkage, 5 per cent.; warps, but not very much; not durable when exposed; hard to work; separates easily in layers, hence used for splints.

COMMON USES: Interior finish, cabinet work, fencing, barrel hoops.

REMARKS: The flexibility of the wood largely determines its uses.

64

OREGON ASH.

Fraxinus oregona Nuttall.

Fraxinus, from a Greek word (phraxis) meaning split, refers to the cleavability of the wood; oregona, named for the State of Oregon.

HABITAT: (See map); best in southern Oregon.

CHARACTERISTICS OF THE TREE: Height, 50'-80'; diameter, 1'-1-1/2', even 4'; branches, stout, erect; bark, grayish brown, deep interrupted fissures, broad, flat ridges, exfoliates; leaves, 5"-14" long; pinnately compound, 5 to 7 leaflets; fruit, single samaras in clusters.

APPEARANCE OF WOOD: Color, brown, sap-wood thick, lighter; ring-porous; rings, plainly marked by large, open, scattered pores; grain, coarse, straight; rays, numerous, thin.

PHYSICAL QUALITIES: Weight, medium (37th in this list); 35 lbs. per cu. ft.; sp. gr., 0.5731; medium strong (50th in this list); elasticity, medium (48th in this list); medium hard (29th in this list); shrinkage, 5 per cent.; warps,............; not durable; hard to work, tough; splits with difficulty.

COMMON USES: Furniture, vehicles, cooperage.

REMARKS: A valuable timber tree of the Pacific coast.

65

BLUE ASH.

Blue, refers to blue dye obtained from inner bark.

Fraxinus quadrangulata Michaux.

Fraxinus, from a Greek word (phraxis) meaning split, refers to the cleavability of the wood; quadrangulata, refers to four-angled branchlets.

HABITAT: (See map); best in lower Wabash valley.

CHARACTERISTICS OF THE TREE: Height, 60'-70', even 120'; diameter, 1'-2'; tall, slender, four-angled, branchlets; bark, light gray, irregularly divided into large plate-like scales, inside bark, bluish, yielding dye; leaves, 8"-12" long, compound pinnate, 5 to 9 leaflets; fruit, winged samaras in panicles.

APPEARANCE OF WOOD: Color, light yellow, streaked with brown, sap-wood lighter; ring-porous; rings, clearly marked by 1 to 3 rows of large, open ducts; grain, straight; rays, numerous, obscure.

PHYSICAL QUALITIES: Heavy (16th in this list); 44 lbs. per cu. ft.; sp. gr., 0.7184; strong (37th in this list); elasticity, medium (58th in this list); hard (12th in this list); shrinkage, 5 per cent.; warps, ...; most durable of the ashes; hard to work; splits readily, bad for nailing.

COMMON USES: Carriage building, tool handles.

REMARKS: Blue ash pitchfork handles are famous.

66

RED ASH.

Red, from color of inner bark.

Fraxinus pennsylvanica Marshall. Fraxinus pubescens Lambert.

Fraxinus, from a Greek word (phraxis) meaning split, refers to the cleavability of the wood; pennsylvanica, in honor of the State of Pennsylvania; pubescens, refers to down on new leaves and twigs.

HABITAT: (See map); best east of Alleghany mountains.

CHARACTERISTICS OF THE TREE: Height, 40'-60'; diameter, 12"-18"; small, slim, upright branches; bark, brown or ashy, great, shallow, longitudinal furrows; leaves, 10"-12" long, pinnately compound, 7 to 9 leaflets, covered with down; fruit, single samara.

APPEARANCE OF WOOD: Color, light brown, sap-wood lighter and yellowish; ring porous; rings, marked by pores; grain, straight, coarse; rays, numerous, thin.

PHYSICAL QUALITIES: Weight, medium (28th in this list); 39 lbs. per cu. ft.; sp. gr., 0.6251; strong (30th in this list); elasticity, medium (53d in this list); hard (17th in this list); shrinkage, 5 per cent.; warps little; not durable; hard to work; splits in nailing.

COMMON USES: Agricultural implements, oars, handles, boats.

REMARKS: Often sold with and as the superior white ash.

67

WHITE ASH.

White, refers to whitish color of wood.

Fraxinus americana Linnaeus.

Fraxinus, from a Greek word (phraxis) meaning split, refers to the cleavability of the wood.

[Illustration: Habitat.]

HABITAT: (See map); best in the bottom lands of lower Ohio valley.

[Illustration: Leaf.]

CHARACTERISTICS OF THE TREE: Height, 70'-80', even 120'; diameter, 3'-6'; branches rather high, tree singularly graceful; bark, gray, narrow furrows, clean, neat trunk; leaves, 8"-15" long, compound, tufted, smooth, turns in autumn to beautiful purples, browns and yellows; fruit, panicles of samaras, persistent till midwinter.

APPEARANCE OF WOOD: Color, light reddish brown, sap-wood whitish; ring-porous, rings clearly marked by pores; straight-grained; pith rays obscure.

PHYSICAL QUALITIES: Heavy (22d in this list); 39 lbs. per cu. ft.; sp. gr., 0.6543; strong (31st in this list); elastic (30th in this list); hard (17th in this list); shrinkage, 5 per cent.; warps little; not durable in contact with soil; hard and tough; splits readily, nails badly.

COMMON USES: Inside finish, farm implements, barrels, baskets, oars, carriages.

REMARKS: Forms no forests, occurs scattered. Its uses for handles and oars determined by combination of strength, lightness and elasticity.

LIST OF 66 COMMON WOODS ARRANGED IN THE ORDER OF THEIR WEIGHT.

1. Shellbark hickory. 2. Post oak. 3. Mockernut. 4. Pignut. 5. Basket oak. 6. Cherry birch. 7. Slash pine. 8. White oak. 9. Bur oak. 10. Western white oak. 11. Western larch. 12. Black locust. 13. Blue beech. 14. Mahogany. 15. Cork

elm. 16. Blue ash. 17. Black oak. 18. Longleaf pine. 19. Hard maple. 20. Beech. 21. Yellow birch. 22. White ash. 23. Red oak. 24. White elm. 25. Sour gum. 26. Oregon maple. 27. Black ash. 28. Red ash. 29. Tamarack. 30. Red maple. 31. Black walnut. 32. Shortleaf pine. 33. Canoe birch. 34. Sweet gum. 35. Wild black cherry. 36. Red birch. 37. Oregon ash. 38. Sycamore. 39. Loblolly pine. 40. Soft maple. 41. Douglas spruce. 42. Red cedar. 43. Norway pine. 44. Western yellow pine. 45. Cucumber tree. 46. Lawson cypress. 47. Black spruce and Red spruce. 48. Bald cypress. 49. Basswood. 50. Chestnut. 51. Black willow. 52. Tideland spruce. 53. Hemlock. 54. Yellow poplar. 55. Redwood. 56. Butternut. 57. White spruce. 58. Western white pine. 59. White pine. 60. Western red cedar. 61. Sugar pine. 62. Grand fir. 63. Engelmann's spruce. 64. White cedar. 65. Big tree.

LIST OF 66 COMMON WOODS ARRANGED IN THE ORDER OF THEIR STRENGTH.

1. Black locust. 2. Yellow birch. 3. Western larch. 4. Cherry birch. 5. Shellbark hickory. 6. Slash pine. 7. Longleaf pine. 8. Hard maple. 9. Blue beech. 10. Beech. 11. Mockernut. 12. Basket Oak. 13. Cork elm. 14. Canoe birch. 15. Pignut hickory. 16. Bur oak. 17. Black oak. 18. Shortleaf pine. 19. Soft maple. 20. Mahogany. 21. Red oak. 22. Red birch. 23. White oak. 24. Tamarack. 25. Lawson cypress. 26. Loblolly pine. 27. Douglas spruce. 28. Western white oak. 29. Post oak. 30. Red ash. 31. White ash. 32. Black walnut. 33. White elm. 34. Sour gum. 35. Wild black cherry. 36. Red maple. 37. Blue ash. 38. Black ash. 39. Norway pine. 40. Western red cedar. 41. Black spruce and Red spruce. 42. White spruce. 43. Red cedar. 44. Hemlock. 45. Western yellow pine. 46. Chestnut. 47. Oregon maple. 48. Bald cypress. 49. Cucumber tree. 50. Oregon ash. 51. Yellow poplar. 52. Sweet gum. 53. Tideland spruce. 54. Sycamore. 55. White pine. 56. Western white pine. 57. Butternut. 58. Redwood. 59. Sugar pine. 60. Basswood. 61. Engelmann's spruce. 62. Grand fir. 63. Big tree. 64. White cedar. 65. Black willow.

LIST OF 66 COMMON WOODS ARRANGED IN THE ORDER OF THEIR ELASTICITY.

1. Western larch. 2. Canoe birch and Yellow birch. 3. Slash pine. 4. Longleaf pine. 5. Hard maple. 6. Cherry birch. 7. Shortleaf pine. 8. Shellbark hickory. 9. Black locust. 10. Douglas spruce. 11. Tamarack. 12. Lawson cypress. 13. Beech.

14. Mockernut. 15. Blue beech. 16. Norway pine. 17. Loblolly pine. 18. Red oak. 19. Red birch. 20. Soft maple. 21. Red spruce and Black spruce. 22. Cork elm. 23. Black walnut. 24. Mahogany. 25. Black oak. 26. Western red cedar. 27. Pignut hickory. 28. Bald cypress. 29. White spruce. 30. White ash. 31. Tideland spruce. 32. White oak. 33. Basket oak. 34. Grand fir. 35. Western white pine. 36. Red maple. 37. Bur oak. 38. Cucumber tree. 39. Yellow poplar. 40. Hemlock. 41. Western yellow pine. 42. Black ash. 43. Sycamore. 44. Sweet gum. 45. Wild black cherry. 46. Chestnut. 47. White pine. 48. Oregon ash. 49. Bass. 50. Post oak. 51. Sour gum. 52. Butternut. 53. Red ash. 54. Western white oak. 55. Engelmann's spruce. 56. Sugar pine. 57. Oregon maple. 58. Blue ash. 59. White elm. 60. Redwood. 61. Red cedar. 62. Big tree. 63. White cedar. 64. Black willow.

LIST OF 66 COMMON WOODS ARRANGED IN THE ORDER OF THEIR HARDNESS.

1. Mahogany. 2. Pignut. 3. Mockernut. 4. Post oak. 5. Shellbark hickory. 6. Black locust. 7. Hard maple. 8. Western white oak. 9. Bur oak. 10. Basket oak. 11. Cherry birch. 12. Blue ash. 13. White oak. 14. Blue beech. 15. Cork elm. 16. Wild black cherry. 17. Red ash. 18. Black oak. 19. White ash. 20. Sour gum. 21. Black walnut. 22. Beech. 23. Black ash. 24. Slash pine. 25. Soft maple. 26. Red oak. 27. Red maple. 28. White elm. 29. Oregon ash. 30. Sycamore. 31. Oregon maple. 32. Yellow birch. 33. Long leaf pine. 34. Red cedar. 35. Western larch. 36. Sweet gum. 37. Red birch. 38. Short leaf pine. 39. Canoe birch. 40. Tamarack. 41. Cucumber tree. 42. Western yellow pine. 43. Loblolly pine. 44. Chestnut. 45. Douglas spruce. 46. Black willow. 47. Butternut. 48. Norway pine. 49. Yellow poplar. 50. Lawson cypress. 51. Hemlock. 52. Bald cypress. 53. Sugar pine. 54. Red spruce and Black spruce. 55. Redwood. 56. Engelmann's spruce. 57. White pine. 58. White spruce. 59. Tideland spruce. 60. Western white cedar. 61. Big tree. 62. White cedar. 63. Western white pine. 64. Basswood. 65. Grand fir.

THE PRINCIPAL SPECIES OF WOODS.

REFERENCES:[A]

Sargent, Jesup Collection. Sargent, Manual. Britton. Roth, Timber. Hough, Handbook. Keeler. Apgar. Mohr. For. Bull., No. 22. Fernow, Forestry

Investigations. Lumber Trade Journals. Baterden. Sargent, Silva. Sargent, Forest Trees, 10th Census, Vol. IX. Boulger. Hough, American Woods. Snow. Lounsberry. Spaulding. For. Bull., No. 13. Sudworth. For. Bull., No. 17. Forest Service Records of Wholesale Prices of Lumber, List. A.

For particular trees consult For. Serv., Bulletins and Circulars. See For. Service Classified List of Publications.

[Footnote A: For general bibliography, see p. 4.]

CHAPTER IV.

THE DISTRIBUTION AND COMPOSITION OF THE NORTH AMERICAN FORESTS.

The forests of the United States, Map, Fig. 44, may be conveniently divided into two great regions, the Eastern or Atlantic Forest, and the Western or Pacific Forest. These are separated by the great treeless plains which are west of the Mississippi River, and east of the Rocky Mountains, and which extend from North Dakota to western Texas.[1]

The Eastern Forest once consisted of an almost unbroken mass, lying in three quite distinct regions, (1) the northern belt of conifers, (2) the southern belt of conifers, and (3) the great deciduous (hardwood) forest lying between these two.

(1) The northern belt of conifers or "North Woods" extended thru northern New England and New York and ran south along the Appalachians. It reappeared again in northern Michigan, Wisconsin and Minnesota. White pine, Fig. 45, was the characteristic tree in the eastern part of this belt, tho spruce was common, Fig. 56, p. 213, and white and Norway pine and hemlock distinguished it in the western part. Altho the more valuable timber, especially the pine, has been cut out, it still remains a largely unbroken forest mainly of spruce, second growth pine, hemlock and some hardwood.

(2) The southern pine forest formerly extended from the Potomac River in a belt from one to two hundred miles wide along the Atlantic coast, across the Florida peninsula, and along the gulf of Mexico, skipping the Mississippi River and reappearing in a great forest in Louisiana and Eastern Texas. It was

composed of almost pure stands of pine, the long-leaf, Fig. 46, the short-leaf, and the loblolly, with cypress in the swamps and bottom lands. In southern Florida the forest is tropical, Fig. 47, like that of the West Indies, and in southern Texas it partakes of the character of the Mexican forest.

(3) Between these north and south coniferous belts, lay the great broad-leaf or hardwood forest, Fig. 48, which constituted the greater part of the Eastern Forest and characterized it. It was divided into two parts by an irregular northeast and southwest line, running from southern New England to Missouri. The southeast portion consisted of hardwoods intermixed with conifers. The higher ridges of the Appalachian Range, really a leg of the northern forest, were occupied by conifers, mainly spruce, white pine, and hemlock. The northwest portion of the region, particularly Ohio, Indiana, and Illinois, was without the conifers. It was essentially a mixed forest, largely oak, with a variable mixture of maples, beech, chestnut, yellow poplar, hickory, sycamore, elm, and ash, with birch appearing toward the north and pine toward the south.

Taking the Eastern Forest as a whole, its most distinguishing feature was the prevalence of broad-leaved trees, so that it might properly be called a deciduous forest. The greatest diversity of trees was to be found in Kentucky, Tennessee and North Carolina, and this region is still the source of the best hardwood lumber.

This great eastern forest, which once extended uninterruptedly from the Atlantic to the Mississippi and beyond, has now been largely lumbered off, particularly thru the middle or hardwood portion, making way for farms and towns. The north and south coniferous belts are still mainly unbroken, and are sparsely settled, but the big timber is cut out, giving place to poorer trees. This is particularly true of the white pine, "the king of American trees," only a little of which, in valuable sizes, is left in Michigan, Wisconsin and Minnesota. In the same way in the south, the long-leaf pine, once the characteristic tree, is fast being lumbered out.

The Western or Pacific forest extends two great legs, one down the Rocky Mountain Range, and the other along the Pacific coast. Between them lies the great treeless alkali plain centering around Nevada, Fig. 49. In these two regions coniferous trees have almost a monopoly. Broad-leaved trees are to be found there, along the river beds and in ravines, but they are of comparatively little importance. The forest is essentially an evergreen forest. Another marked feature of this western forest, except in the Puget Sound region, is that the trees, in many cases, stand far apart, their crowns not even touching, so that the sun beats down and dries up the forest floor, Fig. 50. There is no dense "forest cover" or canopy as in the Eastern Forest. Moreover these western forests are largely broken up, covering but a part of the mountains, many of which are snow-clad, and interrupted by bare plains. Along the creeks there grow a variety of hardwoods. It was never a continuous forest as was the Eastern Forest. The openness of this forest on the Rockies and on the eastern slopes of the Sierra Nevadas is in marked contrast to the western slopes of the Sierras, where there are to be seen the densest and most remarkable woods of the world, Fig. 51. This is due to the peculiar distribution of the rainfall of the region. The precipitation of the moisture upon the northwest coast where the trees are dripping with fog a large part of the time, is unequaled by that of any other locality on the continent. But the interior of this region, which is shut off by the high Sierra Nevadas from the western winds, has a very light and irregular rainfall. Where the rainfall is heavy, the forests are dense; and where the rainfall is light, the trees are sparse.

Along the Rockies the characteristic trees are Engelmann's spruce, bull pine, Douglas fir, and lodgepole pine. As one goes west, the variety of trees increases and becomes, so far as conifers are concerned, far greater than in the east. Of 109 conifers in the United States, 80 belong to the western forests and 28 to the eastern. The Pacific forest is rich in the possession of half a dozen leading species--Douglas fir, western hemlock, sugar pine, bull pine, cedar and redwood.

But the far western conifers are remarkable, not only for their variety, but still more for the density of their growth, already mentioned, and for their great size, Fig. 52. The pines, spruces and hemlocks of the Puget Sound region make eastern trees look small, and both the red fir and the redwood often grow to be over 250 feet high, and yield 100,000 feet, B.M., to the acre as against 10,000 feet, B.M., of good spruce in Maine. The redwood, Fig. 53, occupies a belt some twenty miles wide along the coast from southern Oregon to a point not far north of San Francisco and grows even taller than the famous big trees. The big trees are the largest known trees in diameter, occasionally reaching in that measurement 35 feet.

The big tree, Fig. 54, occurs exclusively in groves, which, however, are not pure, but are scattered among a much larger number of trees of other kinds.

The great and unsurpassed Puget Sound forest is destined to be before long the center of the lumber trade of this country.

These two great forests of the east and the west both run northward into British America, and are there united in a broad belt of subarctic forest which extends across the continent. At the far north it is characterized by the white spruce and aspen. The forest is open, stunted, and of no economic value.

Taking all the genera and species together, there is a far greater variety in the eastern than in the western forests. A considerable number of genera, perhaps a third of the total, grow within both regions, but the species having continental range are few. They are the following: Larch (Larix laricina), white spruce (Picea canadensis), dwarf juniper (Juniperus communis), black willow (Salix nigra), almond leaf willow (Salix amygdaloides), long leaf willow (Salix fluviatilis), aspen (Populus tremuloides), balm of Gilead (Populus balsamifera), and hackberry (Celtis occidentalis).

[Footnote 1: ORIGINAL FOREST REGIONS OF THE UNITED STATES.

Area Area Thousand acres Per cent. Northern forest 158,938 8.4 Hardwood forest 328,183 17.3 Southern forest 249,669 13.1 Rocky Mountains forest 155,014 8.1 Pacific forest 121,356 6.4 Treeless area 887,787 46.7 --------- ----- Total land area 1,900,947 100.0]

THE DISTRIBUTION AND COMPOSITION OF NORTH AMERICAN FORESTS.

REFERENCES:[A]

Sargent, Forest Trees, Intro., pp. 3-10. Bruncken, pp. 5-16. Roth, First Book, pp. 209-212. Shaler, I, pp. 489-498. Fernow, For. Inves., pp. 45-51. Fernow, Economics, pp. 331-368.

[Footnote A: For general bibliography, see p. 4.]

CHAPTER V.

THE FOREST ORGANISM.

The forest is much more than an assemblage of different trees, it is an organism; that is, the trees that compose it have a vital relation to each other. It may almost be said to have a life of its own, since it has a soil and a climate, largely of its own making.

Without these conditions, and without the help and hindrance which forest trees give to each other, these trees would not have their present characteristics, either in shape, habits of growth or nature of wood grain. Indeed, some of them could not live at all.

Since by far the greater number of timber trees grow in the forest, in order to understand the facts about trees and woods, it is necessary to know something about the conditions of forest life.

A tree is made up of three distinct parts: (1) the roots which anchor it in the ground, and draw its nourishment from the moist soil; (2) the trunk, or bole, or stem, which carries the weight of the branches and leaves, and conveys the nourishment to and from the leaves; (3) the crown, composed of the leaves, the branches on which they hang, and the buds at the ends of the branches. As trees stand together in the forest, their united crowns make a sort of canopy or cover, Fig. 55, which, more than anything, determines the factors affecting forest life, viz., the soil, the temperature, the moisture, and most important of all, the light.

On the other hand, every species of tree has its own requirements in respect to these very factors of temperature,--moisture, soil and light. These are called its silvical characteristics.

SOIL.

Some trees, as black walnut, flourish on good soil, supplanting others because they are better able to make use of the richness of the soil; while some trees occupy poor soil because they alone are able to live there at all.

Spruce, Fig. 56, will grow in the north woods on such poor soil that it has no competitors, and birches, too, will grow anywhere in the north woods. In general, it is true that mixed forests, Fig. 57, i.e., those having a variety of species, grow on good loamy soil. The great central, deciduous Atlantic Forest grew on such soil until it was removed to make room for farms. On the other hand, pure stands--i.e., forests made up of single varieties--of pine occupy poor sandy soil. Within a distance of a few yards in the midst of a pure stand of pine in the south, a change in the soil will produce a dense mixed growth of broad-leaves and conifers.

The soil in the forest is largely determined by the forest itself. In addition to the earth, it is composed of the fallen and decayed leaves and twigs and tree trunks, altogether called the forest floor. It is spongy and hence has the ability to retain moisture, a fact of great importance to the forest.

MOISTURE.

Some trees, as black ash and cypress, Fig. 58, and cotton gum, Fig. 59, grow naturally only in moist places; some, as the pinon and mesquite, a kind of locust, grow only in dry places; while others, as the juniper and Douglas fir, adapt themselves to either. Both excessively wet and dry soils tend to diminish the number of kinds of trees. In many instances the demand for water controls the distribution altogether. In the Puget Sound region, where there is a heavy rain-fall, the densest forests in the world are found, whereas on the eastern slopes of the same mountains, altho the soil is not essentially different, there are very few trees, because of the constant drouth.

TEMPERATURE.

The fact that some trees, as paper birch and white spruce, grow only in cold regions, and some, as rubber trees and cypress, only in the tropics, is commonplace; but a fact not so well known is that it is not the average temperature, but the extremes which largely determine the habitat of trees of different kinds. Trees which would not live at all where there is frost, might flourish well in a region where the average temperature was considerably lower. On the other hand, provided the growing season is long enough for the species, there is no place on earth too cold for trees to live. Fig. 60.

In general, cold affects the forest just as poor soil and drought do, simplifying its composition and stunting its growth. In Canada there are only a few kinds of trees, of which the hardwoods are stunted; south of the Great Lakes, there is a great variety of large trees; farther south in the southern Appalachian region, there is a still greater variety, and the trees are just as large; and still farther south in tropical Florida, there is the greatest variety of all. The slopes of a high mountain furnish an illustration of the effect of temperature. In ascending it, one may pass from a tropical forest at the base, thru a belt of evergreen, broad-leaved trees, then thru a belt of deciduous broad-leaved trees, then thru a belt of conifers and up to the timber line where tree life ceases. Figs. 61, and 62.

LIGHT.

More than by any other factor, the growth of trees in a forest is determined by the effect of light. All trees need light sooner or later, but some trees have much more ability than others to grow in the shade when young. Such trees, of which maple and spruce are examples, are called tolerant, while others, for instance, larch, which will endure only a comparatively thin cover or none at all, are called intolerant. The leaves of tolerant trees endure shade well, so that their inner and lower leaves flourish under the shadow of their upper and outer leaves, with the result that the whole tree, as beech and maple, makes a dense shadow; whereas the leaves of intolerant trees are either sparse, as in the larch, or are so hung that the light sifts thru them, as in poplar and oak. The spruces and balsam fir have the remarkable power of growing slowly under heavy shade for many years, and then of growing vigorously when the light is let in by the fall of their overshadowing neighbors. This can plainly be seen in the cross-section of balsam fir, Fig. 63, where the narrow annual rings of the early growth, are followed by the wider ones of later growth. A common sight in the dense woods is the maple sending up a long, spindly stem thru the trees about it and having at its top a little tuft of leaves, Fig. 64. By so doing it survives. The fact that a tree can grow without shade often determines its possession of a burnt-over tract. The order in the North Woods after a fire is commonly, first, a growth of fire weed, then raspberries or blackberries, then aspen, a very intolerant tree whose light shade in turn permits under it the growth of the spruce, to which it is a "nurse," Fig. 65. In general it may be said that all seedling conifers require some shade the first two years, while hardwoods in temperate climates, as a rule, do not.

This matter of tolerance has also much to do with the branching of trees. The leaves on the lower branches of an intolerant tree will not thrive, with the result that those branches die and later drop off. This is called "cleaning," or natural pruning. Intolerant trees, like aspen and tulip, Fig. 66, clean themselves well and hence grow with long, straight boles, while tolerant trees, like spruce and fir, retain their branches longer.

The distribution of a species may also be determined by geographical barriers, like mountain ranges and oceans. This is why the western forests differ radically from the eastern forests and why the forest of Australasia is sharply distinct from any other forest in the world.

Any one or several of these factors, soil, moisture, heat, and light, may be the determining factor in the make-up of a forest, or it may be that a particular tree may survive, because of a faster rate of growth, thus enabling it to overtop its fellows and cut off their light. The struggle for survival is constant, and that tree survives which can take the best advantage of the existent conditions.

Besides these topographical and climatic factors which help determine the distribution of trees, a very important factor is the historical one. For example, the only reason by which the location of the few isolated groves of big trees in California can be accounted for is the rise and fall of glacial sheets, which left them, as it were, islands stranded in a sea of ice. As the glaciers retreated, the region gradually became re-forested, those trees coming up first which were best able to take advantage of the conditions, whether due to the character of their seeds, their tolerance, their endurance of moisture or whatever. This process is still going on and hardwoods are probably gaining ground.

Besides these external factors which determine the composition and organic life of the forest, the trees themselves furnish an important factor in their methods of reproduction. These, in general, are two, (1) by sprouts, and (2) by seeds.

(1) Most conifers have no power of sprouting. The chief exceptions are pitch

pine and, to a remarkable degree, the redwood, Fig. 67. This power, however, is common in broad-leaved trees, as may be seen after a fire has swept thru second growth, hardwood timber. Altho all the young trees are killed down to the ground, the young sprouts spring up from the still living roots. This may happen repeatedly. Coppice woods, as of chestnut and oak, which sprout with great freedom, are the result of this ability. The wood is poor so that it is chiefly used for fuel.

(2) Most trees, however, are reproduced by seeds. Trees yield these in great abundance, to provide for waste,--nature's method. Many seeds never ripen, many perish, many are eaten by animals, many fall on barren ground or rocks, and many sprout, only to die. The weight of seeds has much to do with their distribution. Heavy seeds like acorns, chestnuts, hickory and other nuts, grow where they fall, unless carried down hill by gravity or by water, or scattered by birds and squirrels.

Trees with winged seeds, however, Fig. 68, as bass, maple and pine, or with light seeds, as poplar, often have their seeds carried by the wind to great distances.

Again some trees, as spruce, are very fertile, while others, like beech, have only occasional seed-bearing seasons, once in three or four years. Willow seeds lose their power of germination in a few days, and hence, unless they soon reach ground where there is plenty of moisture, they die. This is why they grow mostly along water courses. On the other hand, black locust pods and the cones of some pines keep their seeds perfect for many years, often until a fire bursts them open, and so they live at the expense of their competitors.

It is such facts as these that help to account for some of the acts of forest composition,--why in one place at one time there is a growth of aspens, at another time pines, at still another oaks; and why beeches spring up one year and not another. That red cedars grow in avenues along fences, is explained by the fact that the seeds are dropped there by birds, Fig. 69.

The fact that conifers, as the longleaf pine, Fig. 46, p. 200, and spruce, Fig. 55, p. 212, are more apt to grow in pure stands than broad-leaved trees, is largely accounted for by their winged seeds; whereas the broad-leaved trees grow mostly in mixed stands because their heavy seeds are not plentifully and widely scattered. This is a rule not without exceptions, for beech sometimes covers a whole mountain side, as Slide Mountain in the Catskills, and aspens come in over a wide area after a fire; but later other trees creep in until at length it becomes a mixed forest.

The essential facts of the relation of trees to each other in the forest has been clearly stated by Gifford Pinchot thus:[1]

The history of the life of a forest is a story of the help and harm which trees receive from one another. On one side every tree is engaged in a relentless struggle against its neighbors for light, water and food, the three things trees need most. On the other side each tree is constantly working with all its neighbors, even those which stand at some distance, to bring about the best condition of the soil and air for the growth and fighting power of every other tree.

The trees in a forest help each other by enriching the soil in which they stand with their fallen leaves and twigs, which are not quickly blown or washed away as are those under a tree in the open. This collection of "duff" or "the forest floor" retains the moisture about their roots, and this moist mass tends to keep the temperature of the forest warmer in winter and cooler in summer. The forest cover, Fig. 55, p. 212, consisting largely of foliage, has the same effect, and in addition protects the bark, the roots, and the seedlings of the trees from the direct and continuous hot rays of the sun. Without the shade of the leaves, many trees, as white pine, would quickly die, as may readily be seen by transplanting them to the open. The mass of standing trees tempers the force of the wind, which might overthrow some of them, and hinders the drying up of the duff.

But trees hinder as well as help each other. There is a constant struggle between them for nourishment and light. To get food and water, some trees, as spruces and hemlocks, Fig. 70, spread their roots out flat; others, as oak and pine, send down a deep tap root. Those succeed in any environment that find the nourishment they need. Still more evident is the struggle for light and air. However well a tree is nourished thru its roots, unless its leaves have an abundance of light and air it will not thrive and make wood.

Even the trees most tolerant of shade in youth, like spruce, must have light later or perish, and hence in a forest there is the constant upward reach. This produces the characteristic "long-bodied" trunk of the forest tree, Fig. 71, in contrast to the "short-bodied" tree of the open, where the branches reach out in all directions, Fig. 72. In this constant struggle for existence is involved the persistent attempt of scattered seeds to sprout whenever there is an opening. The result is that a typical forest is one in which all sizes and ages of trees grow together. Scattered among these are bushes and scrubby trees, called "forest weeds," such as mountain maple and dogwood, Fig. 80, p. 234, which do not produce timber.

By foresters the trees themselves are classified according to their size into:

Seedlings, less than 3' high, Saplings, Small, 3'-10' high. Large, 4" in diameter, at breast height (4' 6"). Poles, Small, 4"-8" in diameter, at breast height. Large, 8"-12" in diameter, at breast height. Standards, 1'-2' in diameter, at breast height. Veterans, over 2' in diameter, at breast height.

Every age has its own dangers. Many seeds never germinate, many seedlings perish because they do not reach soil, or are killed by too much or too little moisture, or by heat or cold, or shade. At the sapling age, the side branches begin to interfere with those of other saplings. Buds are bruised and lower branches broken by thrashing in the wind, and their leaves have less light. Only the upper branches have room and light, and they flourish at the expense of lower ones, which gradually die and are thus pruned off. Some trees naturally grow faster than others, and they attain additional light and room to spread laterally, thus overtopping others which are suppressed and finally killed, beaten in the race for life.

If the growth should remain about even so that the trees grew densely packed together, the whole group would be likely to be of a poorer quality, but ordinarily the few outgrow the many and they are called dominant trees. Even then, they still have to struggle against their neighbors, and at this, the large sapling stage, many perish, and of those that survive there are great differences in size. Trees make their most rapid growth in height, and lay on the widest yearly "rings," at the large sapling and small pole age, Fig. 114, p. 263. It is at this stage, too, if the growth is at all dense, that the young trees (poles) clean themselves most thoroly of their branches. The growth in diameter continues to the end of the tree's life, long after the height growth has ceased.

When trees become "standards," and reach the limit of height growth, thru their inability to raise water to their tops, their branches must perforce grow sidewise, or not at all. The struggle for life thus takes a new form.

How trees are able to raise water as high as they do is still unexplained, but we know that the chief reason why some trees grow taller than others, is due to their ability to raise water. The most remarkable in this respect are the California redwoods, the big trees, and certain eucalypts in Australia. This inability of trees to grow above a certain height results in a flattening of the crown, Fig. 73, and at this stage, the trees struggle against each other by crowding at the side.

Inasmuch as trees grow more sensitive to shade with advancing age, the taller trees have the advantage. Each survivor is one of a thousand, and has outlived the others because it is best fitted for the place.

This fact has its effect upon the next generation, because it is these dominant surviving trees which bear seed most abundantly. After the tree has finished growing in height and diameter most vigorously--the pole stage-- and proved to be fitted for the place, its energy is largely spent in raising seed. As this process goes on generation after generation, only the best coming to maturity in each, the poorer sorts are sifted out, and each region and continent has those species best fitted to meet the conditions of life there.

This is the reason why exotics are very likely to be sensitive and perhaps succumb to influences to which native trees are immune.

Standards and veterans are the survivors of all the lower stages, each of which has had its especial dangers. If left alone, the tree gradually dies and at last falls and decays, adding somewhat to the fertility of the forest soil. From the point of view of human use, it would far better have been cut when ripe and turned into lumber. It is a mistake to suppose that the natural virgin forest is the best possible forest, and that it should therefore be left alone. In the National Forests the ripe lumber is sold and a considerable revenue is thus available. But nature's way with the dead tree is to use it to produce more life. How she does so will be explained in the next chapter, on the enemies of the forest.

[Footnote 1: Gifford Pinchot, Primer of Forestry, p. 44.]

THE FOREST ORGANISM.

REFERENCES:[A]

Pinchot, For. Bull. No. 24, I, pp. 25-66. Bruncken, pp. 13-31. For. Circ. No. 36, p. 8. Fernow, Economics, pp. 140-164.

[Footnote A: For general bibliography, see p. 4]

CHAPTER VI.

NATURAL ENEMIES OF THE FOREST.

The natural enemies of the forest--as distinct from its human enemies--fall into three groups: (1) Meteorological, (2) Vegetable, (3) Animal.

METEOROLOGICAL FORCES.

Wind. "Windfalls" are not an uncommon sight in any forest. Frequently only small areas are blown down, one large tree upsetting a few others, or again a vast region is destroyed by great storms, Fig. 74. An area of many square miles in Florida covered with long-leaf pine was thus destroyed several years ago. The "slash" thus formed, when well dried, is particularly liable to catch fire and burn furiously. Windfalls are especially common among shallow-rooted trees, as hemlock, basswood and spruce, on sandy soil and on shallow soil underlaid with solid stone, especially where open spaces give the wind free sweep. It follows that an unbroken forest is a great protection to itself. The only precautions against wind therefore, that can be taken by the forester, are to keep the forest unbroken by selecting only the larger trees for felling or to cut down a given tract by beginning at the side opposite the direction of prevailing storms and working toward them.

In sandy regions, the wind does immense harm by blowing the sand to and fro in constantly shifting dunes, Figs. 75 and 76. These dunes occupy long stretches of the Atlantic coast and the shore of Lake Michigan. Such dunes have been estimated to cover 20,000 square miles of Europe. Along the Bay of Biscay in France, the sand dunes formerly drifted in ridges along the shore, damming up the streams and converting what was once a forest into a pestilential marsh. This region has been reclaimed at great expense by building fences along the shore to break the wind and thus keep the moving sand within limits. In this way a million acres of productive forest have been obtained.

On the other hand winds are beneficial to the forest in scattering seeds, weeding out weak trees, and developing strength in tree trunks.

Drouth both injures the foliage of trees and causes defects in the grain of wood, the latter appearing as "false rings." These arise from the effort of the tree to resume growth when the water supply is restored. See p. 19.

Water. Certain trees have become accustomed to living in much water, as cedar and cypress have in swamps, and certain trees have become accustomed to periodical floods, but other trees are killed by much water. So when lumbermen make a pond which overflows forest land, the trees soon die, Fig. 77.

Lightning frequently blasts single trees, and in dry seasons may set fire to forests. This is a much more important factor in the west than in the east,--in the Rockies, for instance, where there are electrical storms without rain.

Fires will be considered later under man's relation to the forest.

Snow and ice often bring serious harm to saplings by permanently bending them over, Fig. 78, or by breaking off tops and branches.

Frost kills young plants; and sudden changes in temperature seriously affect grown timber, producing "frost checks" and "wind shakes." When there is a sudden fall in temperature, the outside layers of the tree, which are full of sap, contract more rapidly than the inner portions, with the result that the tree splits with a sudden pistol-like report, the check running radially up and down the tree. This is called a "frost check" or "star shake," Fig. 41.a, p. 47, and such wounds rarely heal, Fig. 79.

On the other hand when the temperature rapidly rises, the outside layers of the tree expand so much more rapidly than the inside, that they separate with a dull muffled chug, the check extending in a circular direction following the annual rings. Such checks are often called "wind shakes" and "cup shakes," Fig. 41.c, p. 47. These injuries are found in regions where sudden changes of temperature occur, rather than in the tropics or in very cold climates.

VEGETABLE ENEMIES.

Under this head may be classed, in addition to fungi, a number of unrelated plants, including such as: moosewood and dogwood, Fig. 80, which crowd out young trees; vines, like bitter-sweet, which wind about trees and often choke them by pressure, cutting thru the bark and cambium; saprophytes, which smother the foliage of trees, of which Spanish moss, Fig. 47, p. 201, is an example; and finally such parasites as the mistletoes, which weaken and deform the trees.

The most important of the vegetable enemies of trees are fungi. It should be remembered, however, that, without the decay produced by them, the fallen trees would soon cover the ground, and prevent any new growth, thus destroying the natural forest.

Every tree, as has been noted (p. 17), is composed of two parts, one part, including leaves, young branches, roots and sap-wood, living, and the other part, namely, the heart-wood, practically dead.

Fungi that attack the live parts of a tree are called parasites, while those that live on dead trunks and branches are designated as saprophytes. The line, however, between these two classes of fungi is not well defined, since some parasites live on both living and dead wood. The parasites are of first importance, for, since they kill many trees, they control to a large extent the supply of living timber.

Nearly all parasitic fungi have two portions, an external fruiting portion which bears the spores--which correspond to the seeds of flowering plants--

and an internal portion consisting of a tangle of threads or filaments, which ramify the tissues of the tree and whose function is to absorb nutriment for the fungus. Fungi are classified botanically according to the spore-bearing bodies, their form, color, etc.

The parasitic fungi which are especially destructive to wood are those that have naked spores growing on exposed fruiting surfaces (the Hymenomycetes). In toadstools (the agarics) these exposed surfaces are thin, flat plates called gills. In the polypores, which include the shelf fungi, the spore surfaces are tubes whose openings constitute the pores. In the dry-rot, or tear fungus (Merulius lacrymans), the spore surfaces are shallow cavities.

Some varieties, called true parasites, develop in uninjured trees, while others, called wound parasites, can penetrate the tissues of trees, only where a cut or injury makes a suitable lodgment for the spores. Some fungi attack only a single species of trees, others whole genera; some attack only conifers, others deciduous trees, while a few attack trees of nearly all kinds alike.

Fungal spores when brought in contact with a wound on a tree or other suitable place, and provided with suitable conditions of growth, germinate, penetrate the tissues and grow very rapidly. These spores send out long threads or filaments which run thru the cells lengthwise and also pierce them in all directions, soon forming a network in the wood called the mycelium.

Rotting, in a large number of cases, is due to the ravages of fungi. This sometimes shows in the color, as the "red rot" of pine or the "bluing" of ash. Sometimes as in "pecky" or "peggy" cypress, the decayed tracts are tubular. More commonly the decayed parts are of irregular shape.

The decay of wood is due to the ravages of low forms of plant life, both bacteria and fungi.

A few of the more destructive forms may be noted.

Trametes pini (Brot.) Fr. Foremost among the timber destroying fungi is the large brown "punk" or "conch" found in its typical development on the long-leaf and short-leaf pines, Pinus palustris and Pinus echinata, Fig. 81. The fruiting bodies form large masses which grow out from a knot, oftentimes as large as a child's head. They are cinnamon brown on the lower surface, and much fissured and broken, on the black charcoal-like upper surface. This fungus probably causes four-fifths of the destruction brought about by the timber destroying fungi. It occurs on most of the conifers in the United States which have any value as lumber trees, and brings about a characteristic white spotting of the wood, Fig. 82, which varies with the kind of tree attacked. (Von Schrenk, Agric. Yr. Bk., 1900, p. 206.)

Of the shelf fungi, which project like brackets from the stems of trees, and have their pores on their under surfaces, one of the commonest in many localities is the yellow cheese-like Polyporus sulphureus, Fig. 83. This is found on oak, poplar, willow, larch, and other standing timber.

Its spawnlike threads spread from any exposed portion of cambium into the pith-rays and between the annual rings, forming thick layers of yellowish-white felt, and penetrating the vessels of the wood, which thereupon becomes a deep brown color and decays.

Of the umbrella-shaped gill-bearing fungi, a yellow toadstool, called the honey mushroom (Agaricus melleus), is a good example, Fig. 84.

This fungus, of common occurrence in the United States as well as in Europe, is exceedingly destructive to coniferous trees, the white pine in particular suffering greatly from its attacks. It also fastens upon various deciduous species as a parasite, attacking living trees of all ages, but living as well upon dead roots and stumps and on wood that has been cut and worked up, occurring frequently on bridges, railroad ties, and the like, and causing prompt decay wherever it has effected an entrance. The most conspicuous part of the fungus is found frequently in the summer and fall on the diseased parts of the tree or timber infested by it. It is one of the common toadstools, this particular species being recognized by its yellowish color, gills extending downward upon the stem, which is encircled a little lower down by a ring, and by its habit of growing in tufts or little clumps of several or many individuals together. It is also particularly distinguished by the formation of slender, dark-colored strings, consisting of compact mycelium, from which the fruiting parts just described arise. These hard root-like strings (called rhizomorphs) extend along just beneath the surface of the ground, often a distance of several feet, and penetrate the roots of sound trees. By carefully removing the bark from a root thus invaded the fungus is seen in the form of a dense, nearly white, mass of mycelium, which, as the parts around decay, gradually produces again the rhizomorphs already described. These rhizomorphs are a characteristic part of the fungus. Occurring both in the decayed wood from which they spread to the adjacent parts, and extending in the soil from root to root, they constitute a most effective agency in the extension of the disease. * * *

External symptoms, to be observed especially in young specimens recently attacked, consist in a change of the leaves to a pale sickly color and often the production of short stunted shoots. A still more marked symptom is the formation of great quantities of resin, which flow downward thru the injured parts and out into the ground. (Forestry Bulletin No. 22, p. 51.)

Of the irregular shaped fungi, one of the most destructive is a true parasite, i.e., one that finds lodgment without help, called Polyporus annosus and also Trametes radiciperda, Fig. 85. It is peculiar in developing its fructifications on the exterior of roots, beneath the soil. Its pores appear on the upper side of the fructifications. It attacks only conifers.

Its spores, which can be readily conveyed in the fur of mice or other burrowing animals, germinate in the moisture around the roots: the fine threads of "spawn" penetrate the cortex, and spread thru and destroy the cambium, extending in thin, flat, fan-like, white, silky bands, and, here and there, bursting thru the cortex in white, oval cushions, on which the subterranean fructifications are produced. Each of these is a yellowish-white, felt-like mass, with its outer surface covered with crowded minute tubes or "pores" in which the spores are produced. The wood attacked by this fungus first becomes rosy or purple, then turns yellowish, and then exhibits minute black dots, which surround themselves with extending soft white patches. (Boulger, p. 73.)

2. Roots of a diseased spruce tree, with numerous small sporophores of polyporus annosus attached. Forestry Bulletin 22, Plate XIII, Figs. 1 and 2.]

Of the fungi which attack converted timber, the most important is "dry rot" or "tear fungus" (Merulius lachrymans), Fig. 86. It flourishes on damp wood in still air, especially around stables and ill ventilated cellars. It gets its name lachrymans (weeping) from its habit of dripping moisture.

The fungus destroys the substance of the timber, lessening its weight and causing it to warp and crack; until at length it crumbles up when dry into a fine brown powder, or, readily absorbing any moisture in its neighborhood, becomes a soft, cheese-like mass. * * * Imperfectly seasoned timber is most susceptible to dry rot: the fungus can be spread either by its spawn or by spores, and these latter can be carried even by the clothes or saws of workmen, and are, of course, only too likely to reach sound wood if diseased timber is left about near it; but on the other hand dry timber kept dry is proof against dry rot, and exposure to really dry air is fatal to the fungus. (Boulger, p. 75.)

[Illustration: Fig. 86. Portion of the mycelium of dry rot or tear fungus, Merulius lachrymans. This cakelike mass spreads over the surface of the timber. In a moist environment pellucid drops or "tears" distil from its lower surface: Hence its name. [Ward: Timber; Fig. 21.]]

About all that can be done to protect the forest against fungi is to keep it clean, that is, to clear out fallen timber and slash, and in some cases to dig trenches around affected trees to prevent spreading or to cut them out and destroy them. Such methods have heretofore been too expensive to employ in any ordinary American forest, but the time is at hand when such action will prove profitable in many localities.

For the preservation of cut timber from decay, several methods are used. Fungi need heat, air, moisture and food. If any one of these is lacking the fungus cannot grow. Air and heat are hard to exclude from wood, but moisture and food can be kept from fungi. The removal of moisture is called seasoning, and the poisoning of the food of fungi is a process of impregnating wood with certain chemicals. Both these processes are described in Handwork in Wood, Chapter III.

ANIMAL ENEMIES.

The larger animals working damage to our forests are chiefly rodents and grazing animals. Beavers gnaw the bark, while mice and squirrels rob the forest of seed and consequently of new trees. The acorns of white oak are particularly liable to be devoured because of their sweetness, while those of red and black oak, which afford timber of comparatively little value, are allowed to sprout, and thus come to possess the land. Hogs annually consume enormous quantities of "mast," i.e., acorns or other nuts, by pasturing in oak and other forests. They, together with goats and sheep, Figs. 87 and 88, deer and cattle, work harm by trampling and browsing. Browsing destroys the tender shoots, especially of deciduous trees, but trampling entirely kills out the seedlings. The cutting up of the soil by the sharp cleft hoofs injures the forest floor, by pulverizing it and allowing it to be readily washed away by storms until deforestation may result, as was the case in France after the Revolution. It has cost the French people from thirty to forty million dollars to repair the damage begun by the sheep. In this country, this matter has become a very serious one on the Pacific Coast, where there are enormous flocks of sheep, and therefore the government is trying to regulate the grazing on public lands there, especially on steep slopes, where erosion takes place rapidly.[1]

[Footnote 1: The evils of grazing are increased by the fact that fires are sometimes started intentionally in order to increase the area of grazing land.]

The most destructive animal enemies of the forest are the insects. The average annual loss of trees in the United States from this cause alone has been estimated to be one hundred million dollars.

Insects have two objects in their attack on trees, one is to obtain food, as when they are in the larval stage, and the other is to provide for offspring, as do certain beetles.

The number of insect enemies of the forest is enormous. At the St. Louis Exposition, there were on exhibit nearly three hundred such insects. These belong to some twenty orders, of which the beetles (Coleoptera), which have horny wings and biting mouth parts, and the moths and butterflies (Lepidoptera), with membraneous wings and sucking mouth parts, are the most destructive. Insects attack every part of the tree, the seed, the shoot, the flower, the root, the leaf, the bark and the wood, both standing and cut.

Of the fruit and seed pests, the most destructive are weevils, worms and gall insects.

Of the twig and shoot pests, beetles, weevils and caterpillars are the worst.

Among insects that attack roots, the periodical cicada (17 year old locust) may be noted.

The leaf pests are far more serious. They include the true and false caterpillars, moths, gall insects and plant lice.

Of the bark pests, the bark beetles are the most destructive. These are also called Engraver Beetles from the smoothly cut figures which are their burrows under the bark, Figs. 89, 90, 91.

Many pairs of beetles make a simultaneous attack on the lower half of the main trunk of medium-sized to large trees. They bore thru the outer bark to the inner living portion, and thru the inner layers of the latter; they excavate long, irregular, longitudinal galleries, and along the sides of these at irregular intervals, numerous eggs are closely placed. The eggs soon hatch and the larvae at once commence to feed on the inner bark, and as they increase in size, extend and enlarge their food burrows in a general transverse but irregular course, away from the mother galleries (see illustration). When these young and larval forms are full grown, each excavates a cavity or cell at the end of its burrow and next to the outer corky bark. (Hopkins, Agric. Yr. Bk., 1902.)

Some of the species attack living trees, causing their rapid death, and are among the most destructive enemies of American forests.

All of the above indirectly affect both the quantity and quality of the wood supply. They can be studied more in detail in the publications of the U.S. Bureau of Entomology.

Of the insects directly attacking wood, the most important are the ambrosia or timber beetles, the borers, the ants, and the carpenter bees. The most remarkable feature of the beetle is the manner of its boring into the harder parts of the wood. Its jaws are particularly constructed for this work, being heavy and strong. The boring is done something after the manner of countersinking, and the jaws are believed to be self-sharpening, by reason of the peculiar right to left and left to right motion.

Ambrosia or timber beetles, Fig. 92. This class of insects attacks living, dead, and felled trees, sawlogs, green lumber, and stave-bolts, often causing serious injury and loss from the pin-hole and stained-wood defects caused by their brood galleries. The galleries are excavated by the parent beetles in the sound sap-wood sometimes extending into the heart-wood, and the young stages feed on a fungus growth which grows on the walls of galleries. (Hopkins, Entom. Bulletin No. 48, p. 10.) The growth of this ambrosia-like fungus is induced or controlled by the parent beetles and the young are dependent on it for food. (Hopkins, Agric. Yr. Bk., 1904.)

There are two general types or classes of these galleries, one in which the broods develop together in the main burrows, the other, in which the individuals develop in short separate side chambers extending at right angles from the primary gallery, Fig. 93. The galleries of the latter type are usually accompanied by a distinct staining of the wood, while those of the former are not. (Hopkins, Agric. Yr. Bk., 1904, p. 383.)

Bark and wood borers, Fig. 94. This class of enemies differs from the preceding in the fact that the parent beetles do not burrow into the wood or bark, but deposit their eggs on the surface. The elongate, whitish, round-headed (Cerambycid), flat-headed (Buprestid), or short, stout (Curculionid) grubs hatching from these eggs cause injury by burrowing beneath the bark, or deep into the sap-wood and heart-wood of living, injured and dead trees, sawlogs, etc. Some of the species infest living trees, Fig. 95, causing serious injury or death. Others attack only dead or dying bark and wood, but this injury often results in great loss from the so-called wormhole defects. (A. D. Hopkins, Entom. Bull., No. 48, p. 10.)

The pine sawyers are among the most troublesome pests in the mill yard, and their large, white larvae often do much damage to logs by eating great holes thru their solid interior. While burrowing in the wood the larvae make a peculiar grating sound that may be heard on quiet nights at a considerable distance. This is a familiar sound in the lumber camps of the North, and has probably given rise to the name of the pine sawyers by which these insects are known. (Forestry Bulletin, No. 22, p. 58.)

Powder-post beetles, Fig. 96. This is a class of insects representing two or three families of beetles, the larvae of which infest and convert into fine powder many different kinds of dry and seasoned wood products, such as hickory and ash handles, wagon spokes, lumber, etc., when wholly or in part from the sap-wood of trees. Oak and hemlock tan-bark is sometimes injured to a great extent, and the structural timbers of old houses, barns, etc., are often seriously injured, while hop poles and like products are attacked by one set of these insects, the adults of which burrow into the wood for the purpose of depositing their eggs. (Hopkins, Forestry Bulletin No. 48, p. 11.)

Timber worms, Fig. 97. This class of true wood-boring "worms," or grubs, are the larvae of beetles. They enter the wood from eggs deposited in wounds in living trees, from which they burrow deep into the heart-wood. Generation after generation may develop in the wood of a tree without affecting its life but the wood is rendered worthless for most purposes by the so-called wormhole and pinhole defects resulting from their burrows. The same species also breed in the wood of dying and dead standing trees, and in the stumps and logs of felled ones, often for many years after the trees are felled. One species sometimes attacks freshly sawed oak lumber, new stave bolts, etc. They are among the most destructive enemies of hardwood forest trees, especially in reducing the value of the wood of the best part of the trunks. (Hopkins, Forestry Bulletin No. 48, p. 10.)

[Illustration: Fig. 97. Work of Timber Worms in Oak: a, Work of oak timber worm, Eupsalis minuta; b. Barked surface; c. Bark; d. Sap-wood timber worm, Hylocaetus lugubris, and its work; e. Sap-wood. [Agric. Year Book, 1904, Fig. 47, p. 386.]]

The carpenter worms, Fig. 98. These are large pinkish caterpillars which are the larvae of stout-bodied moths. They enter the bark and wood of living oak, locust, poplar and other trees, from eggs deposited by the moths in the crevices of uninjured bark, or in the edges of wounds. They burrow deep into the solid wood, where they live for two or three years before transforming to the adult. The wood is seriously injured by the very large wormhole defects, and while the life of the tree is but slightly, if at all, affected by the earlier attacks, the continued operations of this class of borers year after year, finally results in the decay of the heart-wood, or a hollow trunk and a dead top. (Hopkins, Forestry Bulletin, No. 48, p. 11.)

Columbian Timber-beetle One of the commonest wormhole defects in white oak, rock oak, beech, and tulip ("whitewood" or "yellow poplar") is one known to the lumber trade as grease spots, patch-worm, or black holes, Fig. 99, steam boats, Fig. 100, etc., caused by the Columbian timber beetle (Corthylus columbianus Hopk.) The characteristic feature of this wormhole defect, which will enable it to be readily recognized in oak and beech, is transverse series of two or more black holes about the size of the lead in an ordinary lead pencil, with a streak of stained wood extending with the grain two or three or more inches each side, as in Fig. 99. In quarter-sawed oak or split or sawed staves, a short longitudinal section of one of these black holes is seen attended by the stained streak on one side of a thick or curly growth or grain, Fig. 100. It is this form which is called "steamboats." In whitewood (yellow poplar) the black holes are attended by very long black, greenish, or bluish streaks, sometimes five or six feet long. When this is common in the lumber it is called "calico poplar." Fig. 101 represents the characteristic appearance of this defect greatly reduced. (Hopkins, Agric. Yr. Bk., 1903, p. 327.)

Carpenter bees. The work of this class of woodboring bees is shown in Fig. 102. The injury consists of large augerlike tunnels in exposed, solid dry wood of buildings and other structures. It is most common in soft woods, such as pine, poplar, redwood and the like. (Hopkins, Agric. Yr. Bk., 1904, p. 390.)

Horn tails. This is a class of borers which are the larvae of the so-called wood wasps. They may enter the exposed dead wood of wounds of living trees, but more commonly attack the wood of dead standing conifers and hard woods, in the sap-wood of which they excavate irregular burrows, which are packed with their borings. When the adults emerge they leave the surface perforated with numerous round holes. Water and fungi entering these holes cause a very rapid decay of the wood. (Hopkins, Entom. Bull. No. 48, p. 11.)

The tunnels of these various wood pests are most frequently to be seen in chestnut, ash, hickory, oak, tulip, and cypress.

One would think that with such an array of enemies, the forest would hardly survive, but on the other hand there are many enemies of these pests. The most destructive are the predaceous and parasitic insects. Many insects are simply predaceous, pouncing upon and destroying such other insects as they can overcome. Still others are parasites, some external, but most of them living within the bodies of their victims where they pass their entire larval life. The eggs are laid on or in the body of the victim, so that as soon as one hatches, it has suitable food. The ichneumon fly, Fig. 103, is such a parasite; it destroys millions of insect pests. It has a long and peculiar ovipositor with which it drills a hole into the tree and deposits the egg in a burrow of the Pigeon Horntail, a wood wasp that burrows into deciduous trees. The larva soon finds its victim, the grub of the Pigeon Horntail, and lives on it to its destruction.

It would seem that it is a hopeless task to control the insect enemies of forest trees and forest products or to prevent losses from their ravages, but the writer is informed by Dr. A. D. Hopkins, the expert in the Bureau of Entomology in charge of forest insect investigations, that the results of their investigations show conclusively that there are many practical and inexpensive methods of control now available thru the suggestions and recommendations in recent Department publications on forest insects, as well as thru direct correspondence with the Department. These methods are based on the principle of prevention and not on that of extermination. It has been shown that thru proper adjustment of the details in management of forests and of the business of manufacturing, storing, transporting, and utilizing the products a large percentage of the losses can be prevented at small additional expense, and that even when considerable cost is involved the amount saved will often represent a handsome profit.

THE NATURAL ENEMIES OF THE FOREST.

REFERENCES:[A]

(1) Meterological.

Pinchot, Primer I, pp. 75-76. Roth, First Book, pp. 198-202. Bruncken, pp. 27-29.

Water. Roth, First Book, p. 27.

Snow, ice and frost. Pinchot, Primer, I, p. 76. Bruce, For. and Irr., 8: 159, Ap.

'02.

(2) Vegetable.

Roth, First Book, p. 4. Boulger, pp. 70-75. Spaulding, For. Bull., No. 22. Ward, Chaps. V, VI, VII. Sickles, pp. 41-45. von Schrenck, For. Bull., No. 41, Pl. III. Sherfesee. For. Circ. No. 139. von Schrenck, Bur. Plant Ind. Bull. No. 36. von Schrenck, Bur. Plant Ind. Bull. No. 32. von Schrenck, Agric. Yr. Bk., 1900, p. 199.

(3) Animal.

Grazing. Pinchot, Primer I, pp. 69-73, II, p. 73. Pinchot, Agric. Yr. Bk., 1898, p. 187 Coville, For. Bull. No. 15, pp. 28-31. Roth, First Bk., p. 130, 178.

Insects. Comstock, passim. Hopkins, Agric. Yr. Bk., 1902, pp. 265-282. Roth, First Book, pp. 115-130. Howard, Entom. Bull., No. 11, n. s. Hopkins, Spaulding, Entom. Bull., No. 28. Hopkins, Entom. Bull., No. 48. Hopkins, Agric. Yr. Bk., 1903, pp. 313-329. Hopkins, Agric. Yr. Bk., 1904, pp. 382-389, Figs. 43-56. Pinchot, Primer, I, p. 73. Felt, N. Y. State Museum Bull., 103, Ent. 25. Hopkins, Entom. Bull. No. 32. Hopkins, Entom. Bull. No. 56. Hopkins, Entom. Bull. No. 58. Spaulding and Chittenden, For. Bull. No. 22, pp. 55-61.

[Footnote A: For general bibliography, see p. 4.]

CHAPTER VII.

THE EXHAUSTION OF THE FOREST.

The exhaustion of the forest in the United States is due to two main causes: (1) Fire, and (2) Destructive Lumbering.

FIRE.

It is not commonly realized that forest fires are almost entirely the result of human agency. When cruisers first began to locate claims in this country, practically no regions had been devastated by fire. Now such regions are to be seen everywhere. Altho lightning occasionally sets fire to forests, especially in the Rocky Mountains, the losses from this cause are trifling compared with the total loss.

Opportunities for fire. There are a number of facts that make the forest peculiarly liable to fire. Especially in the fall there are great quantities of inflammable material, such as dry leaves, twigs, and duff lying loose ready for ignition. The bark of some trees, as "paper birch," and the leaves of others, as conifers, are very inflammable. It follows that fires are more common in coniferous than in deciduous forests. After lumbering or windfalls, the accumulated "slash" burns easily and furiously, Fig. 104. Moreover a region once burned over, is particularly liable to burn again, on account of the accumulation of dry trunks and branches. See Fig. 107.

Long dry seasons and high wind furnish particularly favorable conditions for fire. On the other hand, the wind by changing in direction may extinguish the fire by turning it back upon its track. Indeed the destructive power of fires depends largely upon the wind.

Causes of fire. Forest fires are due to all sorts of causes, accidental and intentional. Dropped matches, smouldering tobacco, neglected camp fires and brush fires, locomotive sparks, may all be accidental causes that under favorable conditions entail tremendous loss. There is good reason to believe that many forest fires are set intentionally. The fact that grass and berry bushes will soon spring up after a fire, leads sheep men, cattle and pig owners, and berry pickers to set fires. Vast areas are annually burned over in the United States for these reasons. Most fires run only along the surface of the ground, doing little harm to the big timber, and if left alone will even go out of themselves; but if the duff is dry, the fire may smoulder in it a long time, ready to break out into flame when it reaches good fuel or when it is fanned by the wind, Fig. 105. Even these ground fires do incalculable damage to seeds and seedlings, and the safest plan is to put out every fire no matter how small.

Altho it is true that the loss of a forest is not irremediable because vegetation usually begins again at once, Fig. 106, yet the actual damage is almost incalculable. The tract may lie year after year, covered with only worthless weeds and bushes, and if hilly, the region at once begins to be eroded by the rains.

After the fire, may come high winds that blow down the trunks of the trees, preparing material for another fire, Fig. 107.

The statistics of the actual annual money loss of the timber burned in the United States are not gathered. In 1880 Professor Sargent collected much information, and in the census of that year (10th Census, Vol. IX) reported 10,000,000 acres burned that year at a value of $25,000,000.

In 1891, the Division of Forestry collected authentic records of 12,000,000 acres burned over in a single year, at an estimated value of $50,000,000.

In the Adironacks in the spring of 1903, an unprecedentedly dry season, fire after fire caused a direct loss of about $3,500,000.

In 1902, a fire on the dividing line between Washington and Oregon destroyed property amounting to $12,000,000. Within comparatively recent years, the Pacific Coast states have lost over $100,000,000 worth of timber by fire alone.

During September, 1908, forest fires raged in Minnesota, Michigan, Wisconsin, Maine, New York and Pennsylvania. The estimates of loss for northern Michigan alone amounted to $40,000,000. For two weeks the loss was set at $1,000,000 a day. The two towns of Hibbing and Chisholm were practically wiped out of existence, and 296 lives were lost.

Certain forest fires have been so gigantic and terrible as to become historic.

One of these is the Miramichi fire of 1825. It began its greatest destruction about one o'clock in the afternoon of October 7th of that year, at a place about sixty miles above the town of Newcastle, on the Miramichi River, in New Brunswick. Before ten o'clock at night it was twenty miles below New Castle. In nine hours it had destroyed a belt of forest eighty miles long and twenty-five miles wide. Over more than two and a half million acres almost every living thing was killed. Even the fish were afterwards found dead in heaps on the river banks. Many buildings and towns were destroyed, one hundred and sixty persons perished, and nearly a thousand head of stock. The loss from the Miramichi fire is estimated at $300,000, not including the value of the timber. (Pinchot, Part 1. p. 79-80.)

Of such calamities, one of the worst that is on record is that known as the Peshtigo fire, which, in 1871, during the same month, October, when Chicago was laid in ashes, devastated the country about the shores of Green Bay in Wisconsin. More than $3,000,000 worth of property was burnt, at least two thousand families of settlers were made homeless, villages were destroyed and over a thousand lives lost. (Bruncken, p. 110.)

The most destructive fire of more recent years was that which started near Hinckley, Minn., September 1, 1894. While the area burned over was less than in some other great fires, the loss of life and property was very heavy. Hinckley and six other towns were destroyed, about 500 lives were lost, more than 2,000 persons were left destitute, and the estimated loss in property of various kinds was $25,000,000. Except for the heroic conduct of locomotive engineers and other railroad men, the loss of life would have been far greater.

This fire was all the more deplorable, because it was wholly unnecessary. For many days before the high wind came and drove it into uncontrollable fury, it was burning slowly close to the town of Hinckley and could have been put out. (Pinchot, Part I, 82-83.)

One of the most remarkable features of these "crown fires," is the rapidity with which they travel. The Miramichi fire traveled nine miles an hour.

To get an idea of the fury of a forest fire, read this description from Bruncken. After describing the steady, slow progress of a duff fire, he proceeds:

But there comes an evening when nobody thinks of going to bed. All day the smoke has become denser and denser, until it is no longer a haze, but a thick yellowish mass of vapor, carrying large particles of sooty cinders, filling one's eyes and nostrils with biting dust, making breathing oppressive. There is no escape from it. Closing windows and doors does not bar it out of the houses; it seems as if it could penetrate solid walls. Everything it touches feels rough, as if covered with fine ashes. The heat is horrible altho no ray of sunshine penetrates the heavy pall of smoke.

In the distance a rumbling, rushing sound is heard. It is the fire roaring in the tree tops on the hill sides, several miles from town. This is no longer a number of small fires, slowly smouldering away to eat up a fallen log; nor little dancing flames running along the dry litter on the ground, trying to creep up the bark of a tree, where the lichens are thick and dry, but presently falling back exhausted. The wind has risen, fanning the flames on all sides, till they leap higher and higher, reaching the lower branches of the standing timber, enveloping the mighty boles of cork pine in a sheet of flame, seizing the tall poles of young trees and converting them into blazing beacons that herald the approach of destruction. Fiercer and fiercer blows the wind, generated by the fire itself as it sends currents of heated air rushing upward into infinity. Louder and louder the cracking of the branches as the flames seize one after the other, leaping from crown to crown, rising high above the tree tops in whirling wreaths of fire, and belching forth clouds of smoke hundreds of feet still higher. As the heated air rises more and more, rushing along with a sound like that of a thousand foaming mountain torrents, burning brands are carried along, whirling on across the firmament like evil spirits of destruction, bearing the fire miles away from its origin, then falling among the dry brush heaps of windfall or slashing, and starting another fire to burn as fiercely as the first. * * *

There is something horrible in the slow, steady approach of a top fire. It comes on with the pitiless determination of unavoidable destiny, not faster than a man can walk. But there is no stopping it. You cannot fight a fire that seizes tree top after tree top, far above your reach, and showers down upon the pigmy mortals that attempt to oppose it an avalanch of burning branches, driving them away to escape the torture and death that threatens them. (Bruncken, American Forests and Forestry, 106-109.)

Real forest fires are not usually put out; men only try to limit them. A common method of limitation is to cut trenches thru the duff so that the fire cannot pass across, Fig. 108. In serious cases back fires are built on the side of the paths or roads or trenches toward the fire, in the expectation that the two fires will meet. In such cases great care has to be taken that the back fire itself does not escape. Small fires, however, can sometimes be beaten out or smothered with dirt and sand, since water is usually unavailable.

But "an ounce of prevention is worth a pound of cure." One of the best of these preventions is a system of fire lanes. Even narrow paths of dirt will stop an ordinary fire. Roads, of course, are still better. Systems of fire lanes, Fig. 109, are made great use of in Europe and British India. Belts of hardwood trees are also cultivated along railways, and to break up large bodies of conifers.

If in lumbering, the slash were destroyed or even cut up so as to lie near the ground and rot quickly, many fires would be prevented.

Some states, as New York, have a fairly well organized system of fire wardens, who have the authority to draft as much male help as they need at $2.00 a day to fight forest fires. Unfortunately "ne'er-do-wells" sometimes set fire to the woods, in order to "make work" for themselves. Much preventive work is also done by educating the public in schools and by the posting of the fire notices,[1] Fig. 110.

DESTRUCTIVE LUMBERING.

How the reckless and destructive methods of lumbering common in America came into vogue, is worth noting.[2]

The great historical fact of the first half century of our country was the conquest of the wilderness. That wilderness was largely an unbroken forest. To the early settler, this forest was the greatest of barriers to agriculture. The crash of a felled tree was to him a symbol of advancing civilization. The woods were something to be got rid of to make room for farms, Fig. 111. In Virginia, for example, where the soil was soon exhausted by tobacco culture and modern fertilizers were unknown, there was a continual advance into the woods to plant on new and richer land. The forest was also full of enemies to the settler, both animals and Indians, and was a dreaded field for fire. So there grew up a feeling of hate and fear for the forest.

More than that the forest seemed exhaustless. The clearings were at first only specks in the woods, and even when they were pushed farther and farther back from the seacoast, there was plenty of timber beyond.

The idea that the area of this forest could ever be diminished by human hands to any appreciable extent so that people would become afraid of not having woodland enough to supply them with the needed lumber, would have seemed an utter absurdity to the backwoodsman. * * * Thus the legend arose of the inexhaustible supply of lumber in American forests, a legend which only within the last twenty years has given place to juster notions. (Bruncken, p. 57.)

This tradition of abundant supply and the feeling of hostility to the forest lasted long after the reasons for them had disappeared. When we remember that every farm in the eastern United States, is made from reclaimed forest land and that for decades lumber was always within reach up the rivers, down which it was floated, it is not strange that reckless and extravagant methods of cutting and using it prevailed.

Following the settler came the lumberman, who continued the same method of laying waste the forest land. The lumber market grew slowly at first, but later developed by leaps and bounds, until now the output is enormous.

Lumbering in America has come to be synonymous with the clearing off of all the marketable timber, regardless of the future. It treats the forest as tho it were a mine, not a crop, Fig. 112. Since 1880 the total cut has been over 700,000,000 feet, enough to make a one inch floor over Vermont, Massachusetts, Connecticut, Rhode Island and Delaware, or one-half of the State of New York, an area of 25,000 square miles.

Other countries, too, have devastated their forests. Portugal has a forest area of only 5 per cent. of the total land area, Spain and Greece, each 13 per cent., Italy 14 per cent. and Turkey 20 per cent. Whether the destruction of the American forests shall go as far as this is now a live question which has only just begun to be appreciated.

Another reason for the reckless American attitude toward the forest is the frequency and severity of forest fires. This has led to the fear on the part of lumbermen of losing what stumpage they had, and so they have cleared their holdings quickly and sold the timber. Their motto was "cut or lose."

A third incentive to devastative methods was the levy of what were considered unjust taxes.

Hundreds of thousands of acres in the white pine region, notably in Michigan, Wisconsin, and Minnesota, have been cut over, abandoned, sold for taxes, and finally reduced by fire to a useless wilderness because of the shortsighted policy of heavy taxation. To lay heavy taxes on timber land is to set a premium on forest destruction, a premium that is doing more than any other single factor to hinder the spread of conservative lumbering among the owners of large bodies of timber land. * * * Heavy taxes are responsible for the barrenness of thousands of square miles which should never have ceased to be productive, and which must now lie fallow for many decades before they can be counted again among the wealth-making assets of the nation. (Pinchot, Agric. Yr. Bk., 1898, pp. 184-185.)

On the treatment of the questions of fire and taxes depends the future of American forest industries. (Bruncken, p. 226.)

Undoubtedly much waste has been caused by sheer ignorance of forest conditions and methods, which, if followed, would secure successive crops instead of one, but it is safe to say that the desire for immediate profits has been the dominant cause of reckless lumbering. So short-sighted has the policy of private owners proved itself, that it is a question whether any large extent of forest land can safely be left in private hands. No individual lives long enough to reap more than one forest crop. Only corporations and States can be expected to have an interest long enough continued to justify the methods of conservative lumbering.

As a matter of fact, nearly one-half of the privately owned timber of the United States is held by 195 great holders, the principal ones being the Southern Pacific Company, the Weyerhauser Timber Company, and the Northern Pacific Railway Company, which together own nearly 11 per cent. of the privately owned forests of the country. These large holders are cutting little of their timber, their object, however, being not so much to conserve the forests as to reserve to themselves the incalculable private profits which are expected to come with the future enormous increase in the value of timber.

Over against this policy, stands that of the United States Forest Service of increasing the area of the National Forests in order to conserve them for the public welfare. The pity is that the government ever let the forests pass out of its hands. Only forty years ago seventy-five per cent. of the timber now standing was publicly owned. Now about eighty per cent. of it is privately owned. In the meanwhile its value has increased anywhere from ten to fifty fold, according to locality.[3] Some large corporations, however, like the Pennsylvania Railroad, the Kirby Lumber Company, of Texas, and the International Paper Company, have entered upon a policy of conservative lumbering.

Of the actual practices which distinguish destructive lumbering, a few may be cited. Stumps are cut too high and tops too low. Good lumber is wasted on lumber roads and bridges, Fig. 113. Saplings are torn down in dragging out logs. Slash is left in condition to foster fires and left with no shade protection. Seedlings are smothered with slash. Seed trees are all cut out leaving no chance for reproduction. Only poorer sorts of trees are left standing, thus insuring deterioration. Paper pulp cutting goes even farther than lumbering, and ordinarily leaves nothing behind but a howling wilderness.

The production of turpentine from the long-leaf pine, Fig. 114, at the annual rate of 40,000 barrels has meant the devastation of 70,000 acres of virgin forest.

In view of this wholesale destruction it becomes of interest to know how much still remains of the timber supply of the United States. The latest and most authoritative estimate of standing timber in continental United States, excluding Alaska, gives a total of 2,800,000,000 M feet B.M.,[4] of which 2,200,000,000 M feet are privately owned, about 539,000,000 M feet are in the National Forests (Fig. 119, p. 271,) and 90,000,000 M feet are on the unreserved public lands, National parks, State lands and Indian reservations.

Earlier estimates were hardly more than guesses. For example the census of 1880 estimated the stumpage of the U. S. at 856,290,100 M feet, while the census of 1900 gives a total of 1,390,000,000 M feet. The discrepancy appears still greater when it is remembered that in the meantime 700,000,000 M feet were cut. Of this amount 500,000,000 M feet were of conifers or 80,000,000 M feet more than were included in the estimate of 1880. The simple fact is of course that the earlier estimates were gross underestimates, due to the fact that they were based on entirely inadequate data, and therefore can not be used to obscure the now unquestionable fact that the timber supply of this country is surely and rapidly melting away.

The Forest Service estimates that the present annual cut of saw timber is about 50,000,000 M feet. At this rate the present stand would last about 55 years and the privately owned timber only 44 years. This estimate does not allow for growth and decay.

While the population of the United States increased 52 per cent. from 1880 to 1900, during the same period the lumber-cut increased 94 per cent. In other words the yearly increase in use is 20 to 25 per cent. per capita, that is, fast as the population grows, the lumber consumption increases nearly twice as fast. This increase in the lumber-cut far overbalances the growth of trees.

It is also to be remembered that this increase in the use of lumber is in spite of the enormous increase of substitutes for lumber, such as brick, cement and steel for building, and steel for bridges, vehicles, fences, machinery, tools, and implements of all kinds.

How lavishly we use lumber may further be appreciated from the fact that we consume 260 cubic feet[5] per capita, while the average for 13 European countries is but 49 cubic feet per capita. In other words every person in the U. S. is using five times as much wood as he would use if he lived in Europe. It is estimated that on an average each person in this country uses annually the product of 25 acres of forest. The country as a whole, cuts every year, between three and four times more wood than all the forests grow in the meantime. By contrast, the principal countries of Europe, cut just the annual growth, while Russia, Sweden and Japan, cut less than the growth. In other words, the 2,800,000,000,000 feet B.M. of the stumpage of the United States is a capital which is constantly drawn upon, whereas, the 944,700,000,000 board feet of the forest of the German Empire is a capital which is untouched but produces annually 300 board feet per acre.

Southern States include: Virginia, North Carolina, South Carolina, Georgia, Florida, Alabama, Mississippi, Louisiana, Arkansas, Texas and Oklahoma.

Pacific States include: Washington, Oregon and California.

North Atlantic States include: New England, New York, Pennsylvania, New Jersey, Delaware, and Maryland.

Lake States include: Michigan, Wisconsin, and Minnesota.

Central States include: Ohio, West Virginia, Kentucky, Tennessee, Indiana, Illinois, and Missouri.

Rocky Mountain States include: Montana, Idaho, Wyoming, Nevada, Utah, Colorado, Arizona, and New Mexico.]

One striking evidence of the decrease of the timber supply is the shifting of its sources. Once the northeastern States produced over half of the lumber product. They reached their relative maximum in 1870 when they produced 36 per cent. At that time the Lake States produced about 24 per cent. By 1890 the Lake States came to their maximum of 36 per cent. Today the southern States are near their maximum with 41 per cent., but the center will soon shift to the Pacific States. Their product rose from less than 10 per cent. of the whole in 1900 to 17 per cent. in 1908, Figs. 115 and 116. When that virgin forest has been cut off, there will be no new region to exploit; whereas, heretofore, when a region was exhausted, the lumbermen have always had a new one to which to move. At the annual meeting of the Northern Pine Manufacturers' Association in Minneapolis, Minn., January 22, 1907, Secretary J. E. Rhodes made this striking statement:

Since 1895, 248 firms, representing an annual aggregate output of pine lumber of 4-1/4 billion feet, have retired from business, due to the exhaustion of their timber supply. Plants representing approximately 500 million feet capacity, which sawed in 1906, will not be operated in 1907.

The shifting of the chief sources of supply has, of course, been accompanied by a change in the kinds of lumber produced. There was a time when white pine alone constituted one-half of the total quantity. In 1900 this species furnished but 21.5 per cent., in 1904 only 15 per cent., of the lumber cut.[6] We do not use less pine because we have found something better, but because we have to put up with something worse.

The present annual cut of southern yellow pine is about 13-1/4 million M feet, or a little less than one-third of the total cut of all the species. At the present rate of consumption, it is evident that within ten or fifteen years, there will be a most serious shortage of it. Meanwhile the cut of Douglas fir on the Pacific coast has increased from 5 per cent. of the total lumber cut in 1900 to 12 per cent. in 1905. This increase is in spite of the fact, already noted (p. 262) that the great timber owning companies of the northwest are holding their stumpage for an expected great increase in value.

Another evidence of shortage is the almost total disappearance of certain valuable species. Hickory, which once made American buggies famous, is getting very scarce, and black walnut once commonly used for furniture, is available now for only fine cabinet work, veneers, gun stocks, etc. Hardwoods that are fit for the saw are rapidly decreasing. The hardwood cut of 1900 of 8,634,000 M feet diminished in 1904 to 6,781,000 M feet.

A still further evidence of the decreasing supply, is the rising scale of prices. White pine, which sold for $45.00 per M during 1887-1892, sold for $100.00 f.o.b. N. Y., Jan. 1, 1911. Yellow poplar went up in the same period, 1887-1911, from $29.00 to $63.00. Yellow pine rose from $18.00 in 1896 to $47.00 in 1911, and hemlock, the meanest of all woods, from $11.50 in 1889 to $21.00 in 1911, Fig. 118.

The qualities of lumber shown in the above chart are as follows:

White Ash, 1st and 2d, 1" and 1-1/2" x 8" and up by 12'-16'.

Basswood, 1st and 2d, 1" x 8" and up by x 00".

White Oak, quarter-sawed, 1st and 2d, all figured, 1" x 6" and up x 10'-16'.

Yellow poplar, 1st and 2d, 1" x 7"-17" x 12'-16'.

Hemlock, boards

Spruce, No. 1 and clear, 1" and 1-1/4" x 4" x 13'.

White pine, rough uppers, 1" x 8" and up x 00'.

Yellow pine, edge grain flooring. The curve is approximately correct, for the standard of quality has been changed several times.]

It is to be remembered, moreover, that as the timber in any region becomes scarcer, the minimum cutting limit is constantly lowered, and the standard of quality constantly depreciated. Poorer species and qualities and smaller sizes, which were once rejected, are now accepted in the market. For example, 6 inches is now a common cutting diameter for pine and spruce, whereas 12 inches was the minimum limit, and on the Pacific coast there is still nothing cut below 18 inches. This cutting of smaller sizes is largely due to the capacious maw of the pulp mill, which swallows even the poorest stuff. Altho the amount of wood used for paper pulp is small in comparison with the total lumber production, being about 5.4 per cent., yet this cutting of young growth keeps the forest land devastated. In 1906 nearly 9,000,000 tons of wood were used for paper pulp in the United States.

No one who is at all familiar with the situation doubts for an instant that we are rapidly using up our forest capital. In fact it is unquestionably safe to say that our present annual consumption of wood in all forms is from three to four times as great as the annual increment of our forests. Even by accepting the highest estimate of the amount of timber standing we postpone for only a few years the time when there must be a great curtailment in the use of wood, if the present methods of forest exploitation are continued. Every indication points to the fact that under present conditions the maximum annual yield of forest products for the country as a whole has been reached, and that in a comparatively short time, there will be a marked decrease in the total output, as there is now in several items. (Kellogg, Forestry Circular, No. 97, p. 12.)

On the other hand, it is to be remembered that there are influences which tend to save and extend the forest area. These will be considered in the next chapter, on the Use of the Forest.

[Footnote 1:

LOOK OUT FOR FIRE!

RULES AND LAWS.

Fires for clearing land near a forest must not be started until the trees are in full leaf. Before lighting such fires three days' notice, at least, must be given to the Firewarden and occupants of adjoining lands. After such fires are lighted, competent persons must remain to guard them until the fire is completely extinguished, and the persons starting such fires will be held responsible for all damages notwithstanding notice had been given to the Firewarden.

Fires will be permitted for the purposes of cooking, warmth and insect smudges, but before such fires are kindled, sufficient space around the spot where the fire is to be lighted must be cleared from all combustible material; and before the place is abandoned, fires so lighted must be thoroly quenched.

All fires other than those hereinbefore mentioned are absolutely prohibited.

Hunters and smokers are cautioned against allowing fires to originate from the use of firearms, cigars and pipes.

Especial care should be taken that lighted matches are extinguished before throwing them down.

All persons are warned that they will be held responsible for any damage or injury to the forest which may result from their carelessness or neglect.

Girdling and peeling bark from standing trees on state land is prohibited. Fallen timber only may be used for firewood.

All citizens are requested to report immediately any cases which may come to their knowledge of injury to woodlands arising from a violation of these rules.

Then follow quotations from the laws of the state of New York.]

[Footnote 2: For the common methods of logging see Handwork in Wood, Chapter I.]

[Footnote 3: See Summary of Report of the Commissioner of Corporations on the Lumber Industry. February 13, 1911. Washington, D. C.]

[Footnote 4: A board foot is one foot square and one inch thick.]

[Footnote 5: 167 cubic feet equal about 1000 board feet.]

[Footnote 6: Forestry Circular, No. 97.]

THE EXHAUSTION OF THE FOREST

REFERENCES:[A]

(1) Fires.

Bruncken, pp. 183-207. Pinchot, Agric. Yr. Bk., p. 189. Suter, For. Circ. No. 36. U. S. Tenth Census, Vol. IX, p. 491 ff. Pinchot, Primer, pp. 77-88. Roth, First Book, pp. 104-112. Sterling, Agric. Yr. Bk., 1904, p. 133.

(2) Destructive Lumbering.

The Settler's Tradition. Bruncken, pp. 40-59, 94. Roth, First Book, pp. 41-45. Pinchot, Primer, II, p. 82.

Taxation. For. and Irr., April, '06. Pinchot, Agric. Yr. Bk., 1898, p. 184.

Reckless Practices. Pinchot, Primer II, 42-47. Pinchot, Agric. Yr. Bk., 1898, p. 184. Pinchot, For. Circ., No. 25, p. 11. Price, Agric. Yr. Bk., 1902, p. 310. Fox, For. Bull., No. 34, p. 40. Peters, Agric. Yr. Bk., 1905, pp. 483-494. Graves, Agric. Yr. Bk., 1899, p. 415. Suter, For. Bull., 26, pp. 58, 69, 76. Mohr, For. Bull. No. 13, p. 61. Bruncken, pp. 90-98.

The Timber Supply. Kellogg, For. Circ., No. 97 ... Zon, For. Bull., No. 83. Fernow, Economics, pp. 35-45. Report of the Commissioner of Corporations on the Lumber Industry. Part I, Feb. 13, 1911.

[Footnote A: For general bibliography, see p. 4.]

CHAPTER VIII.

THE USE OF THE FOREST.

Man's relation to the forest has not been entirely destructive and injurious. He has exerted and is more and more exerting influences which while still enabling him to use the forest, also preserve and improve it. These activities may all be included under the term Forestry.

The objects of modern forestry then are threefold: 1. The utilization of the forest and its products, the main object; 2. The preservation of the forest, i.e., its continued reproduction; 3. The improvement of the forest.

UTILIZATION.

The uses of the forest are threefold: (1) Protective, (2) Productive, and (3) Esthetic.

(1) Protective. The forest may be used as a protection against floods, wind, shifting sand, heat, drought, etc. The National Forests of the United States, Fig. 119, with the state forests, which include one-fifth of the total forest area, are largely treated as "protection forests" to maintain the head waters of streams, Fig. 120, used for irrigation, for power or for commerce. The attempt now being made to reserve large areas in the White Mountains and southern Appalachians is chiefly for this purpose of protection.

A comparison of Figs. 120 and 121 shows clearly the difference between a region protected by forest and one unprotected.[1]

(2) Productive. All practical foresters have as their first aim the yield of the forest. This distinguishes forestry from landscape architecture, the object of which may equally be the preservation and improvement of a given tract. The crop to be produced is as truly the prime concern of the forester as the raising of agricultural crops is the prime concern of the farmer. It is for this reason that forestry is said to be the same thing as conservative lumbering, Fig. 122. The prejudice of lumbermen against forestry has arisen from a misunderstanding of its aim. Its aim is not to prevent the cutting down of trees, but to direct their cutting in such ways that in the future there will still be trees to cut. "Thru use to a greater use," is the motto of the Forest Service.

The difference between destructive lumbering and conservative lumbering is that the former cuts one crop regardless of the future; while the latter plans to cut crop after crop indefinitely. In other words, in conservative lumbering, the trees to be cut are not selected solely with reference to their immediate market value. Not one crop, but many, is the forester's motto.

So long as the supply seemed exhaustless, forests might be and were treated as mines are, i.e., exploited for the sake of immediate profit; but now that lumbermen begin to realize that the end of the supply is in sight, more conservative methods are being adopted. We cannot afford to kill the goose that lays the golden eggs. In order then to obtain as rich harvests as possible, the modern forester makes use of various methods, some negative, some positive.

Waste is avoided in all possible ways, stumps are cut low and tops high on the trunk, first class trees are not used for skids, bridges, roads, etc., care is taken in "falling" trees and in dragging out logs, that they will not injure other trees. Just as economical disposal of the log has already been carried to a high degree of perfection in the saw-mill, (see Handwork in Wood, Chapter II,) so one object of forestry is to carry this economy back into the woods.

One of the underlying ideas in conservative lumbering is that the "yield," i.e., the amount of wood taken out of a healthy forest in a given time, shall be equal to the amount grown during the same period. If less is taken out than grows, some trees will overmature and decay; if more is taken out than grows, the forest will ultimately be exhausted.

This principle may be carried out in a number of ways; but in any case it is necessary to know how fast the forest is reproducing itself, and this is one of the functions of the forester. The United States Forest Service makes a definite offer of cooperation with farmers and lumbermen and owners of forests to provide them with skilled foresters for direction in this matter.

In the United States, the most practicable way of determining the yield is by area, i.e., a certain fraction of a forest is to be cut over once in a given length of time, a year or longer. The time between two successive cuttings on the same area must be long enough to allow the young trees left standing to ripen.

In a word, conservative lumbering involves (1) the treatment of the forest as a source of crops, (2) systematic gathering, and (3) young growth so left as to replace the outgo.

The important place that forests fill in the national economy may be realized partly by the citation of a few facts as to the forest products. The lumber industry is the fourth in value of products among the great manufacturing industries of the United States, being exceeded only by the iron and steel, the textile, and the meat industries. It turns out a finished product worth $567,000,000.00. And yet lumber constitutes only about one-half of the value of the total output of forest products. Its annual value is three-fourths of a billion dollars, ($666,641,367 in 1907,) while the annual value of wood fuel, is $350,000,000. More than two-thirds of the people burn wood for fuel. The next largest single item in the list is shingles and laths, $32,000,000. (See Forestry Bulletin No. 74, p. 7.)

Outside of food products, no material is so universally used and so indispensable in human economy as wood. (Fernow, Econ., p. 21.)

The importance of forest products may also be learned from a mere list of the varied uses to which they are put. Such a list would include: fuel, wood and charcoal; houses (over half the population of the United States live in wooden houses); the wooden parts of masonry and steel buildings; scaffolding; barns, sheds and outhouses; ships, with all their parts, and the masts and trim of steel ships, boats and canoes; oars and paddles; railway ties (annual expenditure $50,000,000), railway cars, a million in number; trestles and bridges (more than 2,000 miles in length); posts and fencing; cooperage stock (low estimate, $25,000,000 annually); packing crates, including coffins; baskets; electric wire poles (annual cost about $10,000,000); piles and submerged structures, like canal locks and water-wheels; windmills; mining timbers (yearly cost, $7,500,000), indispensable in all mining operations (for every 100 tons of coal mined, 2 tons of mining timber are needed); street paving; veneers ($5,000,000.00 worth made annually); vehicles, including carriages, wagons, automobiles and sleighs; furniture; machines and their parts; patterns for metal molding; tools and tool handles; musical instruments; cigar boxes; matches; toothpicks; pencils; (315 million a year in the U. S., requiring over 7 million cubic feet of wood); engraving blocks; shoe lasts, shoe trees and parts of shoes; hat blocks; agricultural implements; hop and bean poles; playthings and toys, for both children and adults; Christmas trees and decorations; pipes; walking sticks; umbrella handles; crutches and artificial limbs; household utensils; excelsior.

Products other than wood: Turpentine and resin (worth $20,000,000 a year); tar; oils; tan-bark, 1-1/2 million cords (worth $13,000,000 a year); wood alcohol; wood pulp (worth $15,000,000 a year); nuts; cellulose for collars, combs and car wheels; balsam, medicines; lampblack; dyes; paper fiber (xylolin) for textiles; shellac and varnish ($8,500,000 worth imported in 1907); vinegar and acetic acid; confections (including maple sugar and syrup at $2,500,000 a year).

(3) The Esthetic and sentimental uses of the forest, tho not to be estimated in dollars and cents, are nevertheless of incalculable benefit to the community. They would include the use of the forest as pleasure grounds, for hunting, fishing, camping, photography, and general sightseeing. Notable instances of the growing appreciation of these uses of the forest are the reservation of the Yellowstone and Yosemite Parks as pleasure grounds.

PRESERVATION.

The second object of forestry is the preservation of the forest, or continued reproduction.

In addition to obtaining crops of trees, the forester plans to keep the forest in such condition that it will constantly reproduce itself and never become exhausted.

This does not mean that no forests are to be cut down, or that a given area, once a forest, is to be always a forest. Just as the individual farmer needs some land for fields, some for pasture, and some for woodlots, so the nation needs some for cities, some for farms, some for pleasure grounds, and some for forests. But it does mean that fruitful forests shall not be turned into wildernesses as thousands of square miles now are, by the methods of destructive lumbering.

In general, better land is necessary for agriculture than for forestry, and it is therefore only the part of wisdom to use the better land for fields and reserve the poorer land for forests. There are in the United States enormous regions that are fit for nothing but forests, but many of these, as in Wisconsin, Minnesota, and Michigan, have simply been denuded of their trees and no provision has been made for their reproduction. This then is the second aim of forestry,--to treat the forest so that it will continue to reproduce itself.

In order to obtain this result, certain forest conditions have to be preserved. What these conditions are, we have already noticed (see Chap. V, The Forest Organism). They are partly topographical and climatic and partly historical. They include such factors as, soil, moisture, temperature, and light, the forest cover, the forest floor, the density and mixture of growth, all conditions of forest growth. It is only as the forester preserves these conditions, or to put it otherwise, it is only as he obeys the laws of the forest organism that he can preserve the forest. For a long period of our national history, we Americans were compelled to conform our life and institutions to the presence of the primeval forest, but by long observation of what happens naturally in the forest, there have been developed in Europe and in America certain ways of handling it so as to make it our servant and not our master.

These ways are called silvicultural systems. They are all based on the nature of the forest itself, and they succeed only because they are modifications of what takes place naturally in the woods.

As we have seen above (p. 220) trees reproduce themselves either by sprouts or by seeds. This fact gives rise to two general methods of reproduction, called the coppice systems and the seed systems.

Coppice, Fig. 123. In the simpler form of this system, the forest is divided into a certain number of parts, say thirty, and one part is cut down each year. New sprouts at once start up, which will mature a year later than those in the part cut the previous year. Where the trees of each part are thirty years old at cutting, thirty years is called the "rotation period." The coppice is said to be managed on a thirty-year rotation. The system is widely used in eastern United States, for fuel, posts, charcoal, railway ties, and other small stuff, as well as for tan-bark. This system is modified by maintaining an overwood composed of seedling trees or selected sprouts above a stand of sprouts. This is called the Reserve Sprout method and is used with admirable results by the

French.

Seed Forests. In contrast with coppice forests, those raised from seeds produce the best class of timber, such as is used for saw logs.

Seeding from the side, Fig. 124. Many forests naturally spread at their borders from the scattering of their seeds. "Old field pine" is so called from its tendency to spread in this way on old fields. This natural "Seeding from the Side" has given rise to the "Group System," in which an area of ripe trees is cut off and the trees alongside are depended upon to reproduce new ones on the cut-over area. The openings are gradually enlarged until all the old timber is cut out, and the young growth has taken its place. In its best form there is a definite "rotation period," say eighty years. This system is simple, safe, and very useful, especially for small openings in woodlots. A modification of this is the "Strip System," in which long narrow openings, say seventy-five yards wide, are cut out and gradually widened. The strips are cut in the proper direction so that the prevailing winds will cross them, both for the sake of avoiding windfalls and to help scatter the seed. Where the soil is very dry, the strips may run east and west to protect the seedlings from the sun.

Selection Forests. The typical virgin forest, Fig. 125, is one in which trees of all ages are closely intermingled, and it may be either "mixed" or "pure." If a farmer had a woodlot of this character and every year went over it with the ax, cutting out such trees as he needed for his purpose, and also trees whose removal would improve the woods, but taking care not to cut out each year more than the amount of the average growth, he would be using the "Selection System." This system is the best way of keeping a forest dense and of preserving one which is difficult to start afresh, as on a mountain slope; it is practicable where the woods are small or under a high state of care, as in Europe, where this system has been in use for seven centuries. But the cost of road maintenance and of logging is high and it is therefore impracticable in most lumber regions in the United States, except for woods of especial value, like black walnut.

Localized Selection. If instead of the whole forest being treated in this way every year, it were divided up into perhaps twenty parts, and from each part there were taken out each year as much lumber as would equal the annual growth of the whole forest, such a system would be called "Localized

Selection." The cost of logging would be greatly reduced and if care were taken to leave standing some seed trees and to cut no trees below a determined size, as twelve inches, the forest would maintain itself in good condition. This system has been applied with great success in certain private forests in the Adirondacks.

Regular Seed Forest or High Forest. In the system already mentioned above of seeding from the side, the trees near the cut areas are depended upon to seed these areas. Moreover, no especial pains are taken to preserve the forest floor and the forest cover. But all trees do not bear seeds annually, nor do their seedlings thrive under such conditions. In other words, in some forests especial pains must be taken to secure reproduction, and the forest conditions must be maintained with special reference to the growing crop. For this purpose, the cuttings take place thru a series of years, sometimes lasting even twenty years. These reproduction cuttings have reference, now to a stimulus to the seed trees, now to the preparation of the seed bed, now to the encouragement of the seedlings. Then later, the old crop is gradually cut away. Later still, in twenty or thirty years, the new forest is thinned, and when it reaches maturity, perhaps in one hundred or two hundred years, the process is repeated. This is called the "Regular Seed Forest." It produces very valuable timber, and has been used for a long time in Switzerland, especially for beech and balsam.

The system is complicated and therefore unsafe in ignorant hands, and the logging is expensive.

Two-storied Seed Forest. A modification of the system of Regular Seed Forest is the planting of another and a tolerant species of tree under older intolerant trees to make a cover for the soil, to prevent the growth of grass and weeds, and to improve the quality of the upper growth.[2]

An illustration of a natural two-storied seed forest is shown in Fig. 126.

Planting. The planting of forest trees is a comparatively unimportant part of modern forestry. It is a mistaken idea, not uncommon, that the usual way of reproducing forests is to plant trees. It is true that in the pineries of North Germany and in the spruce forests of Saxony, it is common to cut clean and then replant, but it is absurd to conclude, as some have done, that forestry consists of planting a tree every time one is cut. Even if planting were the best method, many more than one tree would have to be planted for each one cut, in order to maintain the forest. So far as America is concerned, not for a long time will planting be much used for reproduction.

The greater portion of American woodlands is in the condition of culled forests, that is, forests from which the merchantable trees have been cut, leaving the younger individuals, as well as all trees belonging to unmarketable species. Even on the areas where the lumbermen have made a clean cut of the original timber, new trees will come up of themselves from seeds blown from the surrounding forests or falling from occasional individuals left standing. (Bruncken, p. 133.)

The usefulness of planting in America is mainly for reclaiming treeless regions, as in the west, and where timber is high priced. The area of planted timber in the Middle West aggregates many hundred thousand acres, once waste land, now converted into useful woods.[3]

Planting has been made possible in the far west by extensive irrigation systems, and farther east by the lessening of prairie fires, which once set the limit to tree growth in the prairie states. In many parts of Illinois, southern Wisconsin and other prairie States, there is much more forest land than there was twenty-five years ago.

What planting can do, may be seen on some worn out pastures in New England, Fig. 127. With the western movement of agriculture, the abandoned farms of New England are to some extent becoming re-forested, both naturally and by planting, as with white pine, which grows even on sandy soil. Between 1820 and 1880, there was a period of enthusiastic white-pine planting in New England, and tho the interest died on account of the cheap transportation of western lumber, those early plantations prove that white pine can be planted at a profit even on sand barrens. Once worn out and useless pastures are now worth $150 an acre and produce yearly a net income of $3 or more an acre.

IMPROVEMENT.

Besides utilization and preservation, the third main object of forestry is the improvement of the forest. It is not an uncommon mistake to suppose that the virgin forest is the best forest for human purposes. It is a comparatively new idea, especially in America, that a forest can be improved; that is, that better trees can be raised than those which grow naturally. Lumbermen commonly say, "You never can raise a second growth of white pine as good as the first growth." As if this "first growth" were not itself the successsor of thousands of other generations! There is even a legend that white pine will not grow in its old habitat. Says Bruncken,

Many people probably imagine that a primeval wood, "by nature's own hand planted," cannot be surpassed in the number and size of its trees, and consequently in the amount of wood to be derived from it. But the very opposite is true. No wild forest can ever equal a cultivated one in productiveness. To hope that it will, is very much as if a farmer were to expect a full harvest from the grain that may spring up spontaneously in his fields without his sowing. A tract of wild forest in the first place does not contain so many trees as might grow thereon, but only so many as may have survived the struggle for life with their own and other species of plants occupying the locality. Many of the trees so surviving never attain their best development, being suppressed, overshadowed, and hindered by stronger neighbors. Finally much of the space that might be occupied by valuable timber may be given up to trees having little or no market value. The rule is universal that the amount and value of material that can be taken from an area of wild forest remains far behind what the same land may bear if properly treated by the forester. It is certain, therefore, that in the future, when most American forests shall be in a high state of cultivation, the annual output of forests will, from a much restricted area, exceed everything known at the present day. (Bruncken, North American Forests and Forestry, pp. 134-135.)

It is probable that the virgin forest produces but a tithe of the useful material which it is capable of producing. (Fernow, p. 98.)

Mr. Burbank has demonstrated that trees can be bred for any particular quality,--for largeness, strength, shape, amount of pitch, tannin, sugar and the like, and for rapidity of growth; in fact that any desirable attribute of a tree may be developed simply by breeding and selecting. He has created walnut trees, by crossing common varieties, that have grown six times as much in thirteen years as their ancestors did in twenty-eight years, preserving at the same time, the strength, hardness and texture of their forebears. The grain of the wood has been made more beautiful at the same time. The trees are fine for fuel and splendidly adapted to furniture manufacture. (Harwood, The New Earth, p. 179.)

Nature provides in the forest merely those varieties that will survive. Man, by interfering in Nature's processes but obeying her laws, raises what he wants. Nature says: those trees that survive are fit and does not care whether the trees be straight or crooked, branched or clear. Man says: those trees shall survive which are fit for human uses. Man raises better grains and fruits and vegetables than Nature, unaided, can, and, in Europe, better trees for lumber. In America there has been such an abundance of trees good enough for our purposes that we have simply gone out and gathered them, just as a savage goes out to gather berries and nuts. Some day our descendants will smile at our treatment of forests much as we smile at root-digging savages, unless, indeed, we so far destroy the forests that they will be more angered than amused. In Europe and Japan, the original supply of trees having been exhausted, forests have been cultivated for centuries with the purpose of raising crops larger in quantity and better in quality.

There are various methods used in forest improvement. Improvement cuttings, as the name implies, are cuttings made to improve the quality of the forest, whether by thinning out poor species of trees, unsound trees, trees crowding more valuable ones, or trees called "wolves"; that is, trees unduly overshadowing others. Improvement cuttings are often necessary as a preliminary step before any silvicultural system can be applied. Indeed, many of the silvicultural systems involve steady improvement of the forest.

The pruning of branches is a method of improvement, carrying on the natural method by which trees in a forest clean themselves of their branches.

Seeds of valuable species are often sowed, when the conditions are proper, in order to introduce a valuable species, just as brooks and ponds are stocked with fine fish. In general it may be said that improvement methods are only in their infancy, especially in America.

[Footnote 1: A concise and interesting statement of the relation of the forest to rain and floods is to be found in Pinchot: Primer of Forestry, Bulletin No. 24, Part II, Chap. III.]

[Footnote 2: For an interesting account of an application of this method, see Ward, p. 35.]

[Footnote 3: To encourage such forest extension, the Forest Service is doing much by the publication of bulletins recommending methods and trees suited to special regions, as, e.g., on Forest Planting in Illinois, in the Sand Hill Region of Nebraska, on Coal Lands in Western Pennsylvania, in Western Kansas, in Oklahoma and adjacent regions, etc.]

THE USE OF THE FOREST.

REFERENCES:[A]

I Utilization.

Pinchot, Primer, II, pp. 14-18, 38-48. Bruncken, pp. 121-131, For. Bull. No. 61.

(1) Protective.

Pinchot, Primer, II, pp. 66-73. Craft, Agric. Yr. Bk., 1905, pp. 636-641, (Map. p. 639.) Toumey, Agric. Yr. Bk., 1903, p. 279. Bruncken, pp. 166-173. For. and Irrig., passim. Shaler, I, pp. 485-489.

(2) Productive.

Kellogg, For. Bull., No. 74, Fernow, For. Invest., p. 9. Roth, First Book, p. 133. Zon & Clark, Agric. Yr. Bk., 1907, p. 277. Boulger, pp. 60-76. Roth, Agric. Yr. Bk., 1896, p. 391. Fernow, Economics, pp. 23-33.

(3) Esthetic.

Roth, First Book, p. 180.

II Preservation.

Pinchot, Primer, II, pp. 18-36. Bruncken, pp. 95, 190. Graves, For. Bull., No. 26, pp. 67-70. Roth, First Book, pp. 41-76, 193-194. Roth, For. Bull., No. 16, pp. 8, 9. Fernow, Economics, 165-196.

Planting.

Roth, First Book, pp. 76-94, 195-198. Hall, Agric. Yr. Bk., 1902, pp. 145-156. For. Circs., Nos. 37, 41, 45, 81. Bruncken, pp. 92, 133. Forestry Bulletins Nos. 18, 45, 52, 65.

III Improvement.

Bruncken, pp. 134-135, 152-160. Graves, For. Bull., No. 26, p. 39. Pinchot, Adirondack Spruce, p. 4. Harwood, pp. 143-181.

[Footnote A: For general bibliography, see p. 4.]

APPENDIX.

HOW TO DISTINGUISH THE DIFFERENT KINDS OF WOOD.[A]

BY B. E. FERNOW AND FILIBERT ROTH.

The carpenter or other artisan who handles different woods, becomes familiar with those he employs frequently, and learns to distinguish them thru this familiarity, without usually being able to state the points of distinction. If a wood comes before him with which he is not familiar, he has, of course, no means of determining what it is, and it is possible to select pieces even of those with which he is well acquainted, different in appearance from the general run, that will make him doubtful as to their identification. Furthermore, he may distinguish between hard and soft pines, between oak and ash, or between maple and birch, which are characteristically different; but when it comes to distinguishing between the several species of pine or oak or ash or birch, the absence of readily recognizable characters is such that but few practitioners can be relied upon to do it. Hence, in the market we find many species mixed and sold indiscriminately.

To identify the different woods it is necessary to have a knowledge of the definite, invariable differences in their structure, besides that of the often variable differences in their appearance. These structural differences may either be readily visible to the naked eye or with a magnifier, or they may require a microscopical examination. In some cases such an examination can not be dispensed with, if we would make absolutely sure. There are instances, as in the pines, where even our knowledge of the minute anatomical structure is not yet sufficient to make a sure identification.

In the following key an attempt has been made--the first, so far as we know, in English literature--to give a synoptical view of the distinctive features of the commoner woods of the United States, which are found in the markets or are used in the arts. It will be observed that the distinction has been carried in most instances no further than to genera or classes of woods, since the distinction of species can hardly be accomplished without elaborate microscopic study, and also that, as far as possible, reliance has been placed only on such characteristics as can be distinguished with the naked eye or a simple magnifying glass, in order to make the key useful to the largest number. Recourse has also been taken for the same reason to the less reliable and more variable general external appearance, color, taste, smell, weight, etc.

The user of the key must, however, realize that external appearance, such, for example, as color, is not only very variable but also very difficult to describe, individual observers differing especially in seeing and describing shades of color. The same is true of statements of size, when relative, and not accurately measured, while weight and hardness can perhaps be more readily approximated. Whether any feature is distinctly or only indistinctly seen will also depend somewhat on individual eyesight, opinion, or practice. In some cases the resemblance of different species is so close that only one other expedient will make distinction possible, namely, a knowledge of the region from which the wood has come. We know, for instance, that no longleaf pine grows in Arkansas and that no white pine can come from Alabama, and we can separate the white cedar, giant arbor vitae of the West and the arbor vitae of the Northeast, only by the difference of the locality from which the specimen comes. With all these limitations properly appreciated, the key will be found helpful toward greater familiarity with the woods which are more commonly met with.

The features which have been utilized in the key and with which--their names as well as their appearance--therefore, the reader must familiarize himself before attempting to use the key, are mostly described as they appear in cross-section. They are:

(1) Sap-wood and heart-wood (see p. 17), the former being the wood from the outer and the latter from the inner part of the tree. In some cases they differ only in shade, and in others in kind of color, the heart-wood exhibiting either a darker shade or a pronounced color. Since one can not always have the two together, or be certain whether he has sap-wood or heart-wood, reliance upon this feature is, to be sure, unsatisfactory, yet sometimes it is the only general characteristic that can be relied upon. If further assurance is desired, microscopic structure must be examined; in such cases reference has been made to the presence or absence of tracheids in pith rays and the structure of their walls, especially projections and spirals.

(2) Annual rings, their formation having been described on page 19. (See also Figs. 128-130.) They are more or less distinctly marked, and by such marking a classification of three great groups of wood is possible.

(3) Spring wood and summer wood, the former being the interior (first formed wood of the year), the latter the exterior (last formed) part of the ring. The proportion of each and the manner in which the one merges into the other are sometimes used, but more frequently the manner in which the pores appear distributed in either.

(4) Pores, which are vessels cut thru, appearing as holes in cross-section, in longitudinal section as channels, scratches, or identifications. (See p. 23 and Figs. 129 and 130.) They appear only in the broad-leaved, so called, hard woods; their relative size (large, medium, small, minute, and indistinct when they cease to be visible individually by the naked eye) and manner of distribution in the ring being of much importance, and especially in the summer wood, where they appear singly, in groups, or short broken lines, in continuous concentric, often wavy lines, or in radial branching lines.

(5) Resin ducts (see p. 26 and Fig. 128) which appear very much like pores in cross-section, namely, as holes or lighter or darker colored dots, but much

more scattered. They occur only in coniferous woods, and their presence or absence, size, number, and distribution are an important distinction in these woods.

(6) Pith rays (see p. 21 and Figs. 129 and 130), which in cross-section appear as radial lines, and in radial section as interrupted bands of varying breadth, impart a peculiar luster to that section in some woods. They are most readily visible with the naked eye or with a magnifier in the broad-leaved woods. In coniferous woods they are usually so fine and closely packed that to the casual observer they do not appear. Their breadth and their greater or less distinctness are used as distinguishing marks, being styled fine, broad, distinct, very distinct, conspicuous, and indistinct when no longer visible by the naked (strong) eye.

(7) Concentric lines, appearing in the summer wood of certain species more or less distinct, resembling distantly the lines of pores but much finer and not consisting of pores. (See Fig. 129.)

Of microscopic features, the following only have been referred to:

(8) Tracheids, a description of which is to be found on page 28.

(9) Pits, simple and bordered, especially the number of simple pits in the cells of the pith rays, which lead into each of the adjoining tracheids.

For standards of weight, consult table on pages 50 and 192; for standards of hardness, table on page 195.

Unless otherwise stated the color refers always to the fresh cross-section of a piece of dry wood; sometimes distinct kinds of color, sometimes only shades, and often only general color effects appear.

[Footnote A: From Forestry Bulletin No. 10, U. S. Department of Agriculture.]

HOW TO USE THE KEY.

Nobody need expect to be able to use successfully any key for the distinction of woods or of any other class of natural objects without some practice. This is especially true with regard to woods, which are apt to vary much, and when the key is based on such meager general data as the present. The best course to adopt is to supply one's self with a small sample collection of woods, accurately named. Small, polished tablets are of little use for this purpose. The pieces should be large enough, if possible, to include pith and bark, and of sufficient width to permit ready inspection of the cross-section. By examining these with the aid of the key, beginning with the better-known woods, one will soon learn to see the features described and to form an idea of the relative standards which the maker of the key had in mind. To aid in this, the accompanying illustrations will be of advantage. When the reader becomes familiar with the key, the work of identifying any given piece will be comparatively easy. The material to be examined must, of course, be suitably prepared. It should be moistened; all cuts should be made with a very sharp knife or razor and be clean and smooth, for a bruised surface reveals but little structure. The most useful cut may be made along one of the edges. Instructive, thin, small sections may be made with a sharp penknife or razor, and when placed on a piece of thin glass, moistened and covered with another piece of glass, they may be examined by holding them toward the light.

Finding, on examination with the magnifier, that it contains pores, we know it is not coniferous or non-porous. Finding no pores collected in the spring-wood portion of the annual ring, but all scattered (diffused) thru the ring, we turn at once to the class of "Diffuse-porous woods." We now note the size and manner in which the pores are distributed thru the ring. Finding them very small and neither conspicuously grouped, nor larger nor more abundant in the spring-wood, we turn to the third group of this class. We now note the pith rays, and finding them neither broad nor conspicuous, but difficult to distinguish, even with the magnifier, we at once exclude the wood from the first two sections of this group and place it in the third, which is represented by only one kind, cottonwood. Finding the wood very soft, white, and on the longitudinal section with a silky luster, we are further assured that our determination is correct. We may now turn to the list of woods and obtain further information regarding the occurrence, qualities, and uses of the wood.

Sometimes our progress is not so easy; we may waver in what group or section to place the wood before us. In such cases we may try each of the doubtful roads until we reach a point where we find ourselves entirely wrong and then return and take up another line; or we may anticipate some of the later mentioned features and finding them apply to our specimen, gain additional assurance of the direction we ought to travel. Color will often help us to arrive at a speedy decision. In many cases, especially with conifers, which are rather difficult to distinguish, a knowledge of the locality from which the specimen comes is at once decisive. Thus, northern white cedar, and bald cypress, and the cedar of the Pacific will be identified, even without the somewhat indefinite criteria given in the key.

KEY TO THE MORE IMPORTANT WOODS OF NORTH AMERICA.

I. NON-POROUS WOODS--Pores not visible or conspicuous on cross-section, even with magnifier. Annual rings distinct by denser (dark colored) bands of summer wood (Fig. 128).

II. RING-POROUS WOODS--Pores numerous, usually visible on cross-section without magnifier. Annual rings distinct by a zone of large pores collected in the spring wood, alternating with the denser summer wood (Fig. 129).

III. DIFFUSE-POROUS WOODS--Pores numerous, usually not plainly visible on cross-section without magnifier. Annual rings distinct by a fine line of denser summer wood cells, often quite indistinct; pores scattered thru annual ring, no zone of collected pores in spring wood (Fig. 130).

NOTE.--The above described three groups are exogenous, i.e., they grow by adding annually wood on their circumference. A fourth group is formed by the endogenous woods, like yuccas and palms, which do not grow by such additions.

I.--NON-POROUS WOODS.

(Includes all coniferous woods.)

A. Resin ducts wanting.[1]

1. No distinct heart-wood.

a. Color effect yellowish white; summer wood darker yellowish (under microscope pith ray without tracheids)..........FIRS.

b. Color effect reddish (roseate) (under microscope pith ray with tracheids) ....HEMLOCK.

2. Heart-wood present, color decidedly different in kind from sap-wood.

a. Heart-wood light orange red; sap-wood, pale lemon; wood, heavy and hard ....YEW.

b. Heartwood purplish to brownish red; sap-wood yellowish white; wood soft to medium hard, light, usually with aromatic odor, ...RED CEDAR.

c. Heart-wood maroon to terra cotta or deep brownish red; sap-wood light orange to dark amber, very soft and light, no odor; pith rays very distinct, specially pronounced on radial section ....REDWOOD.

3. Heart-wood present, color only different in shade from sap-wood, dingy-yellowish brown.

a. Odorless and tasteless ....BALD CYPRESS.

b. Wood with mild resinous odor, but tasteless ....WHITE CEDAR.

c. Wood with strong resinous odor and peppery taste when freshly cut, ...INCENSE CEDAR.

B. Resin ducts present. 1. No distinct heartwood; color white, resin ducts very small, not numerous ....SPRUCE.

2. Distinct heart-wood present.

a. Resin ducts numerous, evenly scattered thru the ring.

a.' Transition from spring wood to summer wood gradual; annual ring distinguished by a fine line of dense summer-wood cells; color, white to yellowish red; wood soft and light ....SOFT PINES.[2]

b.' Transition from spring wood to summer wood more or less abrupt; broad bands of dark-colored summer wood; color from light to deep orange; wood medium hard and heavy ....HARD PINES.[2]

b. Resin ducts not numerous nor evenly distributed.

a'. Color of heart-wood orange-reddish, sap-wood yellowish (same as hard pine); resin ducts frequently combined in groups of 8 to 30, forming lines on the cross-section (tracheids with spirals), ...DOUGLAS SPRUCE.

b'. Color of heart-wood light russet brown; of sap-wood yellowish brown; resin ducts very few, irregularly scattered (tracheids without spirals) ....TAMARACK.

[Footnote 1: Soft and hard pines are arbitrary distinctions and the two not distinguishable at the limit.]

[Footnote 2: To discover the resin ducts a very smooth surface is necessary, since resin ducts are frequently seen only with difficulty, appearing on the cross-section as fine whiter or darker spots normally scattered singly, rarely in groups, usually in the summer wood of the annual ring. They are often much more easily seen on radial, and still more so on tangential sections, appearing there as fine lines or dots of open structure of different color or as indentations or pin scratches in a longitudinal direction.]

====

ADDITIONAL NOTES FOR DISTINCTIONS IN THE GROUP.

Spruce is hardly distinguishable from fir, except by the existence of the resin ducts, and microscopically by the presence of tracheids in the medullary rays. Spruce may also be confounded with soft pine, except for the heart-wood color of the latter and the larger, more frequent, and more readily visible resin ducts.

In the lumber yard, hemlock is usually recognized by color and the silvery character of its surface. Western hemlocks partake of this last character to a less degree.

Microscopically the white pine can be distinguished by having usually only one large pit, while spruce shows three to five very small pits in the parenchyma cells of the pith ray communicating with the tracheid.

The distinction of the pines is possible only by microscopic examination. The following distinctive features may assist in recognizing, when in the log or lumber pile, those usually found in the market:

The light, straw color, combined with great lightness and softness, distinguishes the white pines (white pine and sugar pine) from the hard pines (all others in the market), which may also be recognized by the gradual change of spring wood into summer wood. This change in hard pines is abrupt, making the summer wood appear as a sharply defined and more or less broad band.

The Norway pine, which may be confounded with the shortleaf pine, can be distinguished by being much lighter and softer. It may also, but more rarely, be confounded with heavier white pine, but for the sharper definition of the annual ring, weight, and hardness.

The longleaf pine is strikingly heavy, hard, and resinous, and usually very regular and narrow ringed, showing little sap-wood, and differing in this respect from the shortleaf pine and loblolly pine, which usually have wider rings and more sap-wood, the latter excelling in that respect.

The following convenient and useful classification of pines into four groups, proposed by Dr. H. Mayr, is based on the appearance of the pith ray as seen in a radial section of the spring wood of any ring:

Section I. Walls of the tracheids of the pith ray with dentate projections.

a. One to two large, simple pits to each tracheid on the radial walls of the cells of the pith ray.--Group 1. Represented in this country only by P. resinosa.

b. Three to six simple pits to each tracheid, on the walls of the cells of the pith ray.--Group 2. P. taeda, palustris, etc., including most of our "hard" and "yellow" pines.

Section II. Walls of tracheids of pith ray smooth, without dentate projections.

a. One or two large pits to each tracheid on the radial walls of each cell of the pith ray.--Group 3. P. strobus, lambertiana, and other true white pines.

b. Three to six small pits on the radial walls of each cell of the pith ray. Group 4. P. parryana, and other nut pines, including also P. balfouriana.

====

II.--RING-POROUS WOODS.

(Some of Group D and cedar elm imperfectly ring-porous.)

A. Pores in the summer wood minute, scattered singly or in groups, or in short broken lines, the course of which is never radial.

1. Pith rays minute, scarcely distinct.

a. Wood heavy and hard; pores in the summer wood not in clusters.

a.' Color of radial section not yellow.................ASH.

b.' Color of radial section light yellow; by which, together with its hardness and weight, this species is easily recognized, ...OSAGE ORANGE.

b. Wood light and soft; pores in the summer wood in clusters of 10 to 30 ....CATALPA.

2. Pith rays very fine, yet distinct; pores in summer wood usually single or in short lines; color of heart-wood reddish brown; of sap-wood yellowish white; peculiar odor on fresh section ....SASSAFRAS.

3. Pith rays fine, but distinct.

a. Very heavy and hard; heart-wood yellowish brown. BLACK LOCUST.

b. Heavy; medium hard to hard.

a.' Pores in summer wood very minute, usually in small clusters of 3 to 8; heart-wood light orange brown. RED MULBERRY.

b.' Pores in summer wood small to minute, usually isolated; heart-wood cherry red ....COFFEE TREE.

4. Pith rays fine but very conspicuous, even without magnifier. Color of heart-wood red; of sap-wood pale lemon ...HONEY LOCUST.

B. Pores of summer wood minute or small, in concentric wavy and sometimes branching lines, appearing as finely-feathered hatchings on tangential section.

1. Pith rays fine, but very distinct; color greenish white. Heart-wood absent or imperfectly developed ....HACKBERRY.

2. Pith rays indistinct; color of heart-wood reddish brown; sap-wood grayish to reddish white ....ELMS.

C. Pores of summer wood arranged in radial branching lines (when very crowded radial arrangement somewhat obscured).

1. Pith rays very minute, hardly visible ....CHESTNUT.

2. Pith rays very broad and conspicuous ....OAK.

D. Pores of summer wood mostly but little smaller than those of the spring wood, isolated and scattered; very heavy and hard woods. The pores of the spring wood sometimes form but an imperfect zone. (Some diffuse-porous woods of groups A and B may seem to belong here.)

1. Fine concentric lines (not of pores) as distinct, or nearly so, as the very fine pith rays; outer summer wood with a tinge of red; heart-wood light reddish brown ....HICKORY.

2. Fine concentric lines, much finer than the pith rays; no reddish tinge in summer wood; sap-wood white; heart-wood blackish ....PERSIMMON.

====

ADDITIONAL NOTES FOR DISTINCTIONS IN THE GROUP.

Sassafras and mulberry may be confounded but for the greater weight and hardness and the absence of odor in the mulberry; the radial section of mulberry also shows the pith rays conspicuously.

Honey locust, coffee tree, and black locust are also very similar in appearance. The honey locust stands out by the conspicuousness of the pith rays, especially on radial sections, on account of their height, while the black locust is distinguished by the extremely great weight and hardness, together with its darker brown color.

The ashes, elms, hickories, and oaks may, on casual observation, appear to resemble one another on account of the pronounced zone of porous spring wood. (Figs. 129, 132, 135.) The sharply defined large pith rays of the oak exclude these at once; the wavy lines of pores in the summer wood, appearing as conspicuous finely-feathered hatchings on tangential section, distinguish the elms; while the ashes differ from the hickory by the very conspicuously defined zone of spring wood pores, which in hickory appear more or less interrupted. The reddish hue of the hickory and the more or less brown hue of the ash may also aid in ready recognition. The smooth, radial surface of split hickory will readily separate it from the rest.

1. Pores in the summer wood more or less united into lines.

a. The lines short and broken, occurring mostly near the limit of the ring ....WHITE ASH.

b. The lines quite long and conspicuous in most parts of the summer wood ....GREEN ASH.

2. Pores in the summer wood not united into lines, or rarely so.

a. Heart-wood reddish brown and very firm ....RED ASH.

b. Heart-wood grayish brown, and much more porous ....BLACK ASH.

In the oaks, two groups can be readily distinguished by the manner in which the pores are distributed in the summer wood. (Fig. 133.) In the white oaks the pores are very fine and numerous and crowded in the outer part of the summer wood, while in the black or red oaks the pores are larger, few in number, and mostly isolated. The live oaks, as far as structure is concerned, belong to the black oaks, but are much less porous, and are exceedingly heavy and hard.

====

III.--DIFFUSE-POROUS WOODS.

(A few indistinctly ring-porous woods of Group II, D, and cedar elm may seem to belong here.)

A. Pores varying in size from large to minute; largest in spring wood, thereby giving sometimes the appearance of a ring-porous arrangement.

1. Heavy and hard; color of heart-wood (especially on longitudinal section) chocolate brown ....BLACK WALNUT.

2. Light and soft; color of heart-wood light reddish brown BUTTERNUT.

B. Pores all minute and indistinct; most numerous in spring wood, giving rise to a lighter colored zone or line (especially on longitudinal section), thereby appearing sometimes ring-porous; wood hard, heart-wood vinous reddish; pith rays very fine, but very distinct. (See also the sometimes indistinct ring-porous cedar elm, and occasionally winged elm, which are readily distinguished by the concentric wavy lines of pores in the summer wood) ....CHERRY.

C. Pores minute or indistinct, neither conspicuously larger nor more numerous in the spring wood and evenly distributed.

1. Broad pith rays present.

a. All or most pith rays broad, numerous, and crowded, especially on tangential sections, medium heavy and hard, difficult to split. ....SYCAMORE.

b. Only part of the pith rays broad.

a.' Broad pith rays well defined, quite numerous; wood reddish white to reddish ....BEECH.

b.' Broad pith rays not sharply defined, made up of many small rays, not numerous. Stem furrowed, and therefore the periphery of section, and with it the annual rings sinuous, bending in and out, and the large pith rays generally limited to the furrows or concave portions. Wood white, not reddish ....BLUE BEECH.

2. No broad pith rays present.

a. Pith rays small to very small, but quite distinct.

a.' Wood hard.

a." Color reddish white, with dark reddish tinge in outer summer wood ....MAPLE.

b." Color white, without reddish tinge ....HOLLY.

b.' Wood soft to very soft.

a." Pores crowded, occupying nearly all the space between pith rays.

a.'" Color yellowish white, often with a greenish tinge in heart-wood ....TULIP POPLAR. CUCUMBER TREE.

b.'" Color of sap-wood grayish, of heart-wood light to dark reddish brown ....SWEET GUM.

b." Pores not crowded, occupying not over one-third the space between pith rays; heart-wood brownish white to very light brown ....BASSWOOD.

b. Pith rays scarcely distinct, yet if viewed with ordinary magnifier, plainly visible.

a.' Pores indistinct to the naked eye.

a." Color uniform pale yellow; pith rays not conspicuous even on the radial section .....BUCKEYE.

b." Sap-wood yellowish gray, heart-wood grayish brown; pith rays conspicuous on the radial section. SOUR GUM.

b.' Pores scarcely distinct, but mostly visible as grayish specks on the cross-section; sap-wood whitish, heart-wood reddish ....BIRCH.

D. Pith rays not visible or else indistinct, even if viewed with magnifier.

1. Wood very soft, white, or in shades of brown, usually with a silky luster ....COTTONWOOD (POPLAR).

====

ADDITIONAL NOTES FOR DISTINCTIONS IN THE GROUP.

Cherry and birch are sometimes confounded, the high pith rays on the cherry on radial sections readily distinguishes it; distinct pores on birch and spring wood zone in cherry as well as the darker vinous-brown color of the latter will prove helpful.

Two groups of birches can be readily distinguished, tho specific distinction is not always possible.

1. Pith rays fairly distinct, the pores rather few and not more abundant in the spring wood: wood heavy, usually darker, CHERRY BIRCH and YELLOW

BIRCH.

2. Pith rays barely distinct, pores more numerous and commonly forming a more porous spring wood zone; wood of medium weight, CANOE OR PAPER BIRCH.

The species of maple may be distinguished as follows:

1. Most of the pith rays broader than the pores and very conspicuous ....SUGAR MAPLE.

2. Pith rays not or rarely broader than the pores, fine but conspicuous.

a. Wood heavy and hard, usually of darker reddish color and commonly spotted on cross-section ....RED MAPLE.

b. Wood of medium weight and hardness, usually light colored. SILVER MAPLE.

Red maple is not always safely distinguished from soft maple. In box elder the pores are finer and more numerous than in soft maple. The various species of elm may be distinguished as follows:

1. Pores of spring wood form a broad band of several rows; easy splitting, dark brown heart ....RED ELM.

2. Pores of spring wood usually in a single row, or nearly so.

a. Pores of spring wood large, conspicuously so WHITE ELM.

b. Pores of spring wood small to minute.

a.' Lines of pores in summer wood fine, not as wide as the intermediate spaces, giving rise to very compact grain ROCK ELM.

b.' Lines of pores broad, commonly as wide as the intermediate spaces ....WINGED ELM.

c. Pores in spring wood indistinct, and therefore hardly a ring-porous wood
..................................CEDAR ELM.

[Illustration:

Fig. 138. Wood of Elm. a red elm; b, white elm; c, winged elm.]

[Illustration: Fig. 139. Walnut. p.r., pith rays; c.l., concentric lines; v, vessels or pores; su. w., summer wood; sp. w., spring wood.]

[Illustration: Fig. 140. Wood of Cherry.]